TRAINING PARAPROFESSIONALS FOR REFERENCE SERVICE

A How-To-Do-It Manual for Librarians®

Second Edition

PAMELA J. MORGAN

HOW-TO-DO-IT MANUALS®
NUMBER 164

WITHDRAWN

NEAL-SCHUMAN PUBLISHERS, INC.
New York   London

Published by Neal-Schuman Publishers, Inc.
100 William St., Suite 2004
New York, NY 10038

This Second Edition is a revision of *Training Paraprofessionals for Reference Service: A How-To-Do-It Manual for Librarians,* by Julie Ann McDaniel and Judith K. Ohles, published by Neal-Schuman Publishers in 1993. Copyright © 1993 Julie Ann McDaniels and Judith K. Ohles.

Printed and bound in the United States of America.

The paper used in this publication meets the minimum requirements of American National Standard for Information Sciences—Permanence of Paper for Printed Library Materials, ANSI Z39.48-1992.

Library of Congress Cataloging-in-Publication Data

Morgan, Pamela J.
  Training paraprofessionals for reference service : a how-to-do-it manual for librarians / Pamela J. Morgan. — 2nd ed.
      p. cm. — (How-to-do-it manuals ; no. 164)
  Rev. ed. of : Training paraprofessionals for reference service / Julie Ann McDaniel. 1st ed. 1993.
  Includes bibliographical references and index.
  ISBN 978-1-55570-643-2 (alk. paper)
  1. Reference services (Libraries)—Study and teaching—United States. 2. Library technicians—Training of—United States. I. McDaniel, Julie Ann. Training paraprofessionals for reference service. II. Title.

Z711.2.M36 2009
025.5'2071173—dc22   2008037497

CONTENTS

LIST OF FIGURES

PREFACE

Add new services; sustain existing service levels; and simultaneously manage to maintain (or even reduce) existing budgets.

Every library's reference department is more than familiar with this mantra. Many met this challenge by hiring paraprofessionals to provide reference service. Practically, this staffing tactic has been embraced as a cost-saving measure; philosophically, the practice has been decried as undermining the library profession and providing patrons with a disservice. Staffing a reference desk with paraprofessionals need not compromise library service, but hiring good paraprofessionals is a partial solution. The paraprofessionals must be trained in order for libraries to provide a high level of service. *Training Paraprofessionals for Reference Service*, Second Edition, is intended to serve as a training guide for libraries using paraprofessionals in reference services, from designing the training cycle, to needs assessment to performance evaluation.

This second edition of *Training Paraprofessionals for Reference Service* has been revised to incorporate the changes in reference librarianship since the publication of the first edition in 1993, many of which have been brought on with the advent of the Internet: virtual reference, increasing use of electronic resources, the move to single-service points, an increase of self-services for patrons, the decrease in ready reference questions, and the general appearance of new technologies. The book's sample training materials have been updated to reflect these changes and include modules on online searching, evaluating Internet sources, providing virtual reference, the importance of a library's Web page, and more. Like its predecessor, this edition is still grounded in the traditional values of reference librarianship, stressing the necessity for good communication, knowledge of sources, and demonstrating a willingness to help.

The book is organized into ten chapters, beginning with the process of making the decision to use paraprofessionals at the reference desk. It then progresses through the training cycle: assessment of training needs, design and development of training, implementation, concluding with evaluation of training.

Chapter 1, "Paraprofessionals at the Reference Desk," presents the pros and cons of using paraprofessionals at the reference desk. Even if an organization has already made the decision to use or is already using paraprofessionals at the reference desk, reviewing the con arguments can ensure that libraries avoid some of the pitfalls that could deter them from using support staff.

Chapter 2, "Laying the Groundwork," guides libraries through the steps that must be taken before creating a training plan. Libraries must decide why the reference department needs the paraprofessional and clearly delineate the roles of the professional and paraprofessionals in providing reference service. Because it is the backbone of the training needs, there is information on writing a job description. Finally, in order to ensure a consistent level of quality service, the chapter describes formulating performance expectations and determining guidelines for referral so that "handoffs" from paraprofessionals to professionals are smoothly executed.

Chapter 3, "Creating a Training Plan," provides the nuts and bolts of the training. Included are instructions for pinpointing training needs based on the job description, prioritization of those needs, the formulation of goals and objectives, and determining training content. Suggestions are given for selecting training methods and choosing and creating materials. Because libraries know best what skills and resources their reference staff must master, there is a section on creating training checklists and modules.

Chapter 4, "Orientation," covers an important first step in training—providing an employee's first impression of an organization and laying a foundation upon which training is built. Failure to provide proper orientation could waylay the best-laid training plans. This chapter goes beyond the general orientation that most libraries will have in place for employees and provides tips on orientation to the reference department.

Chapter 5, "Basic Skills," consists of checklists for possible skills that a paraprofessional should learn as quickly as possible to become a contributing member of the reference department. These checklists cover online catalog training, Web services, evaluating Internet sources, and call number training for both Library of Congress and the Dewey Decimal Classification Systems.

Chapter 6, "Advanced Skills," takes the basic skills further, introducing more complex tasks such as online searching skills (including Boolean searching, phrase searching, and keyword searching), link resolvers, federated searching, and Superintendent of Documents (SuDoc) numbers. These skills were selected because many of them are now routinely used within library reference services to locate information. Others (online searching and SuDoc numbers) are more difficult and should be taught only when basic skills are mastered.

Chapter 7, "Ready Reference Skills," presents six modules, which serve as examples of training materials. These modules are designed to instruct a paraprofessional on the use of the specific sources, not how to answer the questions. The sources in this chapter are a subset of available reference sources; individual libraries will have a better idea of what sources are best for training in their particular library. The "Checklists for Designing Modules" in Chapter 3 will assist libraries in developing customized training to meet the information needs of their patrons.

Chapter 8, "Communication Skills," presents basic communication skills to be used in answering routine questions, discusses how to ensure that deceptively simple questions are handled appropriately, and provides guidance on how to refer. For the advanced paraprofessional, there is a section on conducting the reference interview. Differences between in-person, phone, and electronic communication are described.

Chapter 9, "Performance Management," provides guidance on how to maintain the behavior introduced in training and how to develop those skills further. Libraries that invest the time and personnel in training will want to ensure that what was learned will be kept up. This chapter discusses and provides a checklist for meeting performance standards, providing feedback, coaching, and the formal evaluation of performance.

Chapter 10, "Evaluation and Revision of Training," completes the training cycle. Libraries will want see how successful the training was and make changes if necessary. This chapter helps libraries answer several questions in order to assess the training. How did the paraprofessional react to the training? Did he or she acquire the knowledge and skills necessary for good job performance? Did job performance improve as a result of training? Did the training produce the desired results? And finally, what are the next steps for training?

Paraprofessionals should complement, not compete, with professional librarians. *Training Paraprofessionals for Reference Service* addresses the real role that paraprofessionals play in providing reference service, which, for many libraries, has moved beyond the physical desk. The intent of the book is not to suggest that paraprofessionals entirely replace professional librarians at the reference desk, but to work alongside professionals to provide library patrons with the best possible service. However, this requires careful thought, discussion, and planning on the part of the library.

This manual will guide libraries through those necessary steps and can help in a variety of staffing situations: libraries that are considering using paraprofessionals, libraries that will be using paraprofessionals but are unsure how to begin, libraries that are cross-training staff from other areas to help in providing public service, libraries that are consolidating service points (such as an Information Commons, where technological and reference assistance co-exist, even blend), and libraries that make use of student assistants at the desk. Even non-MLS staff who do not work at a desk but might interact with the public (the classic example is the "shelvers" who get asked questions in the book stacks) can benefit from learning about basic communication and referral skills.

Training Paraprofessionals for Reference Service draws on material from the fields of librarianship, instructional design, human resources, training, and staff development. The author hopes that if your library is reinventing, rethinking, or reorganizing reference service, this book will help you make the most of existing and future staff in providing reference service for the twenty-first century.

ACKNOWLEDGMENTS

Many people were instrumental when I was writing Training Paraprofessionals for Reference Service, Second Edition: my two editors at Neal-Schuman, Elizabeth Lund and M. Sandra Wood, who guided me through this entire process; Charles Harmon of Neal-Schuman who provided thoughtful insight and suggestions; the entire staff of the Public Services Department of the Amelia Gayle Gorgas Library at the University of Alabama, in particular my immediate colleagues Maryellen Allen, Barbara Dahlbach, Valerie Glenn, Jennifer McClure, Brett Spencer, and Lisa Yuro. I profited immensely from work and discussions with these six individuals.

I am grateful also to the authors of the first edition, Julie Ann McDaniel and Judith K. Ohles, whose sound scholarship and clear writing provided an excellent base on which to build.

I also wish to thank Gorgas Information Services' graduate assistants Jane Daugherty, Anna Ellis, Faith White, and Sara Maurice Whitver. Working alongside these library school students provided me the opportunity to learn and reflect about the content of the book, not to mention inspiration. I also thank my former colleagues Mark Andersen, Linda Dausch, and Paul Keith, and especially Kathleen Weibel, who helped make this happen.

Last, but not least, I thank my parents and my brother.

1 PARAPROFESSIONALS AT THE REFERENCE DESK

INTRODUCTION

Professional reference librarians today are involved in a number of duties: bibliographic instruction, collection development, liaison work, programming and outreach, committee work, research and publication, supervision and management, and other projects. In addition to these activities, libraries are also rethinking traditional services, such as adding information/learning commons, providing virtual reference, merging service points, and reducing the role of, if not altogether eliminating, the reference desk. As new services are added and old ones revamped, libraries must consider alternative staffing models. One model, which is widely used, is to utilize paraprofessionals to assist with reference service, freeing professional librarians for other duties.

What is meant by "paraprofessional"? The prefix *para* means "by the side of." For example, paramedics or paralegals work with medical and legal professionals. In libraries, the word "paraprofessional" generally refers to an employee who does not have a Master of Library Science (MLS) degree, but who has been trained to work alongside a professional librarian. There are numerous job titles, some of which are roughly synonymous with the term paraprofessional. These job titles include support staff, paralibrarians, aides, assistants, associates, and technicians. The term "preprofessional" is sometimes applied to those who are working toward attaining the MLS degree. Some libraries also use the term "subprofessional" or "nonprofessional" to distinguish librarians from other staff (Johnson, 1996). The "Library Support Staff Resource Center" portion of the American Library Association's Web site (www.ala.org/ala/hrdr/librarysupportstaff/library_support_staff_resource_center.cfm) provides a comprehensive list of job titles. Paraprofessional is the term used throughout the book to refer to library employees who do not have an MLS. This includes workers such as student assistants, graduate assistants, and other support staff who may work at the reference desk.

Libraries using paraprofessionals to provide both technical and public services, including reference, is not a new trend. Murfin and Wynar's annotated bibliography of reference services refers to discussions about the use of paraprofessionals at the desk beginning in the mid-1960s (1977).

Paraprofessional personnel is:

"A term used to designate library employees without professional certification or entrance-level educational requirements who are assigned supportive responsibilities at a high level and commonly perform their duties with some supervision by a professional staff member" (Young, 1983, p. 164).

Fast Facts

The 2008–2009 *Occupational Outlook Handbook* (OOH) predicts that job opportunities for professional librarians to "grow slower than the average" (increase 3 to 6 percent), for the time period ending in 2016. Conversely, for the same time period, the number of jobs for library technicians is expected to "grow about as fast as the average" (increase 7 to 13 percent).

The literature discusses use of non-MLS employees locating basic bibliographic information, and answering directional question (Murfin and Wynar, 1977). One survey, administered in the mid-1970s, found that over two-thirds of 141 libraries at four-year accredited colleges and universities used nonprofessionals to provide reference service (Boyer and Theimer, 1975). A later survey, administered in the mid-1980s, concluded that paraprofessionals were used to staff a reference desk during evenings, weekends, nonpeak hours, and at other times such as conferences (Courtois and Goetsch, 1984). In the 1990s, some libraries began to move toward "tiered" reference (sometimes known as the Brandeis model, after the institution that first proposed this model), a system whereby support staff or graduate students answer simple questions and refer more complex questions to professional librarians (Rettig, 1996). Marcella Genz notes that the debate over whether professionals should answer directional questions, what constitutes the division of labor between support staff and professionals, along with what the reference service model should be began in the 1960s and extended well until the late 1990s (Genz, 1998). A survey administered to major academic libraries in 2000 indicated that many libraries used paraprofessionals to staff the reference desk and handle less complex queries (Jackson, 2002).

The practice of utilizing paraprofessionals in libraries is unlikely to decrease; the *Occupational Outlook Handbook* (U.S. Department of Labor, www.bls.gov/oco) forecasts that budget issues and technology will cause libraries to replace librarians with "library technicians" in many areas, including user services. The American Library Association has recognized the importance of non-MLS support staff in libraries with the creation of the Library Support Staff Interests Round Table (LSSIRT) in 1993. Moreover, questions today still persist about what the appropriate staffing model for reference service should be. Bell (2007), in an article titled "Who Needs a Reference Desk?", proposes eliminating the reference desk altogether and suggests new models of service (roving and consultations). The author admits to the difficulty of doing away with the reference desk, stating, "an academic library without a reference desk staffed by professionals is nearly unthinkable" (Bell, 2007, p. 1). A compromise would have the desk staffed by well-trained paraprofessionals who could answer directional questions, serve as the central help desk, and intercept and refer research questions to professional librarians. Many libraries do not have the luxury of debating who should staff the reference desk. Paraprofessional staff may work at a reference desk out of sheer necessity; at smaller libraries *all* staff provides what service is required as long as the doors are open.

Utilizing paraprofessionals to provide reference service is not without controversy. There have been numerous studies measuring paraprofessionals' effectiveness at the reference desk and patron satisfaction with that service. The articles all make the following point: organizations that choose to use paraprofessionals for reference work must be prepared to invest professional time and proper training in the effort. The decision to make use of paraprofessionals must be made carefully; analysis may reveal that it is ineffective to employ paraprofessionals at the reference desk. There should be a plan as to how paraprofessional staff fit into the overall service model of the library. Once the needs of the library have been determined, it is necessary to develop a plan for hiring, training, supervising, and evaluating paraprofessionals. Only with thorough and ongoing training will paraprofessionals be able to provide high quality service at the reference desk.

> "Reference services traditionally have been plagued by two major areas of inefficiency: librarians spend a lot of time at the desk not answering questions, and librarians spend a lot of time answering questions that don't require their level of training and expertise" (Coffman and Saxton, 1999, p. 142).

ARGUMENTS FOR USING PARAPROFESSIONALS

REDIRECT PROFESSIONAL EXPERTISE

Even prior to the Internet, both articles and presentations in the library science field indicated that many of the transactions at the reference desk did not require professional attention. Some studies estimated that as many as 80 percent of the questions asked at reference desks did not require professional attention (Emmick, 1985). With the advent of Internet search engines, the number of queries requiring professional attention further declined, especially ready reference questions, i.e., questions that tend to request brief, factual information that can be quickly answered utilizing one or two sources. What has increased is the complexity of reference queries. Patrons turn to the reference librarian after they feel they have exhausted their options, and these complex questions require a lengthier, one-on-one consultation (Zabel, 2005a). These complex questions require careful thought in order to construct search strategies and research plans. With the reference desk serving as the place for directional questions and requests for computer and printing help, there is some question as to whether the reference desk is the appropriate location to handle such queries; a suggested alternative is a private office or consultation space (LaGuardia, 2003). Carefully trained paraprofessionals could staff the reference desk to handle routine questions and tasks, freeing professional librarians for other duties and proper attention to more multifaceted queries (Katz, 2002).

COST SAVINGS

Sadly, many libraries are being faced with stagnant or declining operating budgets and must explore new staffing models and/or cost savings (Zabel, 2005b). With ready reference decreasing, it might prove more cost effective to hire paraprofessionals to staff the reference desk. Many libraries wish to hire professionals but simply cannot, due to a shortage of qualified applicants; these libraries must turn to using paraprofessionals (Napier, 2003). In other cases, libraries are under pressure to extend hours either by a few hours per week and/or to "24/7" during certain times of the year. In such cases, the well-trained paraprofessional can facilitate increased hours or keep the doors of the library open.

COMBINED SERVICE POINTS

Due to shifting patterns in library use (e.g., reference transactions are in decline, patrons' greater use of self-check machines, etc.), many libraries are moving toward consolidating service points. A library's decision to combine service points is likely to result in paraprofessionals working alongside reference librarians to provide assistance with technology, circulation, interlibrary loan, reserves, etc. Regardless of what form the single service desk takes or why it exists, training is a critical to the success of that service point. In order to maintain basic levels of service, staff at the combined service desk will need some form of cross-training. The paraprofessional's breadth and depth of reference expertise does not need to be that of the professional librarian, but some sort of competency should be required to maintain service levels (Mozenter, Sanders, and Bellemy. 2003). Cross-training benefits the patron in that there is a larger pool of staff available to answer a wide range of information questions (Allegri and Bedard, 2006).

RESPOND TO CHANGING PATRON NEEDS

Many patrons expect different types of services and expertise from reference desks. One reason is the advent of computer work stations in libraries, which provides access to a variety of tools: the library catalog and databases, productivity software (word processing, spreadsheets, etc.), and communication software. Many users are often multitasking, searching for information alongside with creating it. Patrons require help in a variety of areas and often do not distinguish between traditional library help and computer support; they might ask for in-depth assistance with: spreadsheet formulas; complex headers and footers; uploading, downloading, and transferring files; digital imaging, etc. A variety of expertise is needed. Paraprofessionals at a reference desk can help respond to the technology questions as well as answer basic reference questions. Their presence can also ensure that in-depth research questions are referred to professional librarians. Staff with a wide range of know-how at the reference desk ensure the following:

- Faster and more timely service (patrons are not shuttled between service points)

- Basic reference services and more hours
- Efficient and flexible staffing solutions (Flanagan and Horowitz, 2000)

ARGUMENTS AGAINST USING PARAPROFESSIONALS

VALUE OF PROFESSIONAL EDUCATION

Use of paraprofessionals at reference desks is widespread. This has spawned the fear that the practice will devalue the library profession. The profession sends contradictory messages, "'Come to the desk, where you'll be helped by professionals—experts in finding information' But we also say 'Well-trained paraprofessionals do a fine job at the reference desk. You won't be able to tell the difference between us'" (Lipow, 2003, p. 32). Another concern is that the practice robs patrons of the "highest level of service to all library users" (McKinzie, 2002). Ideally, paraprofessionals should be hired only to complement, not replace, professional librarians; unfortunately, this is not always the case. It is imperative that libraries that choose to use paraprofessionals at the reference desk provide adequate and ongoing training in order to maintain high service levels.

INACCURATE REFERRALS

Some argue that paraprofessionals do not make referrals or do not realize when it is necessary to make a referral to a professional. There is concern that paraprofessionals feel, because they are asked, that they are required to provide assistance, even when it is not appropriate. The reluctance to refer patrons to a professional might also be a face-saving measure; staff fear appearing ignorant to the patron. The difficulty of supervising reference work raises concerns about the success of the reference interview and referrals. In the case of cataloging and interlibrary loan work, the supervisor need not be immediately present to proof and correct. Reference service, however, is not always well suited to close supervision or correction. The immediate and individual nature of reference work makes it difficult to ensure that every question is answered correctly. If a professional librarian must be assigned to watch every transaction in which a paraprofessional is involved, no professional time has been gained. However, if the paraprofessional is allowed to answer questions without training, the quality of service may be lowered because of faulty reference interviewing, improper referrals, or incorrect answers. Some libraries may choose to set up guidelines governing the use of paraprofessionals at reference desks. For example, policy may be written requiring that paraprofessionals always work with a librarian, or that the librarian receives all questions and then refers appropriate questions to the paraprofessional. Paraprofessionals may be allowed to answer only directional, ready reference, and "known item" queries, or they may be asked to get a patron started and then confer with a librarian to determine if the complete, correct answer was given. Guidelines such as these can help avoid inaccurate referrals.

TIME TO TRAIN AND SUPERVISE

The decision not to use a paraprofessional might arise from a cost benefit analysis. Is it worth the professional time to provide ongoing training and supervision of paraprofessionals? There is the issue of staff turnover; paraprofessionals, who may take a library position only until they can obtain higher-level jobs or work in the subject fields, may not remain long enough to justify their training. High turnover can greatly increase the time spent in the hiring and training process. In libraries where the paraprofessional staff is small and has a low rate of turnover, the hiring and training of paraprofessionals will be infrequent and less time-consuming. In libraries with larger staffs and high turnover, one librarian may need to devote some or all of his or her time to training and supervising paraprofessionals. Libraries with small staff and high turnover may need to have stricter guidelines about what paraprofessionals may answer, such as directional and equipment-related questions only.

MAKING THE DECISION

Despite the arguments against the practice, many libraries realize that using paraprofessionals is an effective way of maximizing their services and better utilizing professional staff. Each library must make its own conclusions about using paraprofessionals at its reference desk. It can be helpful to ask the following questions when making the decision:

- How important is contact between a professional librarian and the public at the reference desk? Are there better places and methods for professional librarians to connect with patrons?
- What is the best way to ensure that a paraprofessional is capable of the reference interview?

- Are professionals wasting time answering directional and ready reference questions?
- Would the use of paraprofessionals inhibit patrons from asking for assistance because they feel support staff is incapable of answering a question? (St. Clair, Aluri, and Pastine, 1977)

Concerns about proper referrals and lack of familiarity with reference sources can be overcome if the library hires carefully, sets clear expectations for service provided by paraprofessionals, and follows up with thorough and ongoing training. It is important to realize, however, that these tasks require a considerable amount of planning and effort from the library's professional staff. The library must decide whether the benefits—realizing cost savings, adding new services, increasing hours, freeing its professional staff for other work, or some combination—are worth the professional time commitment to plan, train, and supervise the paraprofessional. Each library must also decide what type and level of questions are appropriate for paraprofessionals to answer and how much education the position should require. The question is usually not whether to use paraprofessionals at the reference desk, but how to use them.

Ultimately, it is the professional librarians who are responsible for the service offered in their library, regardless of who provides the service. Paraprofessionals cannot simply be given a manual and turned loose on the service desk. They need carefully planned training by professionals to orient them to the library, familiarize them with library philosophy, policies and procedures, and guide them in using reference resources, answering questions, and making referrals. Only when this has occurred can libraries uphold the Code of Ethics of the American Library Association, which calls for "the highest level of service to all library users . . . and accurate, unbiased, and courteous responses to all requests."

> "No single answer exists to the question of whether one should use paraprofessionals at the reference desk. Quality of service remains the bottom line in making the decision . . ." (Montag, 1986, p. 36).

REFERENCES

Allegri, Francesca, and Martha Bedard. 2006. "Lessons Learned from Single Service Point Implementations." *Medical Reference Services Quarterly* 25, no. 2 (Summer): 31–47. Provides advice on merging service points, including staffing, referrals, and role of support staff.

Bell, Steven J. 2007. "Who Needs a Reference Desk?" *Library Issues* 27, no. 6 (July): 1–4. Bell proposes libraries get rid of the reference desk and explore new models of providing reference service. He also presents the pros and cons of having a reference desk.

Boyer, Laura M., and William C. Theimer, Jr. 1975. "The Use and Training of Nonprofessional Personnel at Reference Desks in Selected College and University Libraries." *College & Research Libraries* 36, no. 3 (May): 193–200. Presents results from a survey about the use and training of nonprofessional personnel (including student assistants) in academic libraries.

Coffman, Steve, and Matthew L. Saxton. 1999. "Staffing the reference desk in the largely-digital library." *Reference Librarian* no. 66: 142.

Courtois, Martin P., and Lori A. Goetsch. 1984. "Use of Nonprofessionals at Reference Desks." *College & Research Libraries* 45, no. 5 (September): 385–391. Courtois and Goetsch present the results of a survey conducted to determine library use of nonprofessionals at reference desks. The articles also discusses use patterns and desk hours staffed by nonprofessionals, referral and training, and trends for desk staffing.

Emmick, Nancy J. 1985. "Nonprofessionals on Reference Desks in Academic Libraries." In "Conflicts in Reference Services," edited by Bill Katz and Ruth A. Fraley. *The Reference Librarian* no. 12 (Spring/Summer): 149–160. Emmick provides philosophical and practical reasons for and against using paraprofessionals at the reference desk. Although from 1985, many of her points remain valid.

Flanagan, Pat, and Lisa R. Horowitz. 2000. "Exploring New Service Models: Can Consolidating Public Service Points Improve Response to Customer Needs?" *Journal of Academic Librarianship* 26, no. 5 (September): 329–338. Presents how one library combined reference and circulation desks. Especially useful are the sections describing cross training and making referrals.

Genz, Marcella D. 1998. "Working the Reference Desk." *Library Trends* 46, no. 3: 505–525. Marcella Genz examines how the role of reference workers at libraries has evolved and the division of labor between professional librarians and support staff at the reference desk.

Jackson, Rebecca. 2002. "Revolution or Evolution: Reference Planning in ARL Libraries." *Reference Services Review* 30, no. 3: 212–228. Rebecca Jackson discusses the results of a survey administered to Association of Research Library members, including how reference service is being provided and staffed.

Johnson, Peggy. 1996. "Managing Changing Roles: Professional and Paraprofessional Staff in Libraries." *Journal of Library Administration* 22, no. 2/3: 79–99. Johnson examines the changing responsibilities of professional and paraprofessional library staff in academic libraries.

Katz, William A. 2002. "Reference Service Policies and Evaluation" In *Introduction to Reference Work: Volume Two: Reference Services and Reference Processes.* 8th ed. 183–210. NY: McGraw Hill. In his latest (and last) textbook, William Katz discusses the very real issue of burnout and offers solutions that incorporate using paraprofessionals.

LaGuardia, Cheryl. 2003. "The Future of Reference: Get Real!" *Reference Services Review* 31, no. 1: 39–42. Among the fives issues that LaGuardia addresses is the increase in reference question complexity. She also offers her opinion about the role of the professional librarian.

Lipow, Anne Grodzins. 2003. "The Future of Reference: Point-of-Need Reference Service: No Longer an Afterthought." *Reference Services Review* 31, no. 1: 31–35. In her articles sketching out a future scenario of reference services, Grodzins includes observations and criticism about the reference desk.

McKinzie, Steve. 2002. "For Ethical Reference, Pare the Paraprofessionals." *American Libraries* 33, no. 9 (October): 42. Steve McKinzie argues against the use of paraprofessionals to provide reference service, stating the practice violates the American Library Association's Code of Ethics.

Montag, John. 1986. "Choosing How to Staff the Reference Desk" in "Personnel Issues in Reference Services" ed. Bill Katz, Ruth A. Fraley, *The Reference Librarian* no. 14 (Spring/Summer): 36.

Mozenter, Frada, Bridgette T. Sanders, and Carol Bellemy. 2003. "Perspectives on Cross-Training Public Service Staff in the Electronic Age: I Have to Learn to Do What?!" *Journal of Academic Librarianship* 29, no. 6 (November): 399–404. Describes a reorganization of staff and functions in an academic library and the cross-training that followed.

Murfin, Marjorie E., and Lubomyr R. Wynar. 1977. *Reference Service: An Annotated Bibliographic Guide*. Littleton, CO: Libraries Unlimited. Chapter 5, "Reference Service: Non-professional Personnel and Duties," summarizes the professional literature covering the use of paraprofessionals in reference work.

Napier, Alan. 2003. "Spare—Don't Pare—The Paraprofessionals." *American Libraries* 34, no. 4 (April): 38. Alan Napier provides a rebuttal to Steve McKinzie and lists reasons supporting using paraprofessionals at the reference desk.

Rettig, James. 1996. "Future Reference—'Sired by a Hurricane, Dam'd by an Earthquake.'" *Reference Librarian* no. 54: 75–94. James Rettig examines internal and external impacts on providing reference service and discusses tiered reference service.

St. Clair, Jeffrey W., Rao Aluri, and Maureen Pastine. 1977. "Staffing the Reference Desk: Professionals or Nonprofessionals?" *Journal of Academic Librarianship* 3, no. 3 (July): 149–153. Jeffrey W. St. Clair and Rao Aluri analyze questions asked at the reference desk to determine how many could be answered by a nonprofessional staff member. The conclusion is that carefully trained paraprofessionals could handle many of the questions. Maureen Pastine offers a response to the findings, raising questions and implications if a library chooses to use paraprofessionals at the reference desk.

United States Department of Labor. Bureau of Labor Statistiscs. *Occupational Outlook Handbook, 2008–2009 Edition.* Available: www.bls.gov/oco (accessed July 24, 2008). The sections on "Librarians" and "Library Technicians" provide a job outlook and employment projections for both occupations.

Young, Heartsill (ed.). 1983. *The ALA Glossary of Library and Information Science.* Chicago, IL: American Library Association.

Zabel, Diane. 2005a. "Trends in Reference and Public Services: Librarianship and the role of RUSA: Part One." *Reference and User Services Quarterly* 45, no. 1 (Fall): 7–10. Diane Zabel discusses recent trends in reference librarianship. She notes the decrease in the volume of reference questions together with the increase in complexity. She also opines what those trends could mean for staffing.

Zabel, Diane. 2005b. "Trends in Reference and Public Services: Librarianship and the Role of RUSA: Part Two." *Reference and User Services Quarterly* 45, no. 2 (Winter): 104–107. In Part Two, Diane Zabel explores four trends that impact delivery of library services.

ADDITIONAL RESOURCES

The following articles provide background on the decision to use paraprofessionals at the reference desk and detail how training was implemented.

Brandys, Barbara, Joan Daghita, and Susan Whitmore. 2002. "Raising the Bar or Training Library Technicians to Assume Reference Responsibilities." In *SLA 2002: Putting Knowledge to Work. Papers Presented at the Special Libraries Association Conference.* Los Angeles, California, June 9–12, 2002.

Graves, Karen J. 1998. "Implementation and Evaluation of Information Desk Services Provided by Library Technical Assistants." *Bulletin of the Medical Library Association* 86, no. 4 (October): 475–485.

Hammond, Carol. 1992. "Information and Research Support Services: The Reference Librarian and the Information Paraprofessional." *Reference Librarian* no. 37: 91–104.

Lichtenstein, Art A. 1999. "Surviving the Information Explosion: Training Paraprofessionals for Reference Service." *Journal of Educational Media & Library Sciences* 37, no. 2: 125–134.

Pedzich, Joan. 2000. "Paraprofessionals at the Reference Desk: Training and Documentation." *Legal Reference Services Quarterly* 18, no. 2: 91–99.

2 LAYING THE GROUNDWORK

Once the decision has been made to utilize paraprofessionals, the library must determine exactly what the employee will do, create a job description for the position(s), and establish performance standards for the staff member. Taking these steps will lay the groundwork necessary to design a training plan. This chapter covers assessment, writing a job description, and determining performance standards.

ASSESSMENT

Before creating a job description for a paraprofessional, several questions need to be addressed. What role will the position play in the reference department? Will the paraprofessionals be part-time student workers at the reference desk or full-time persons with a bachelor's degree? What activities at the reference desk require professional attention and which do not? Will the paraprofessional only answer ready reference and directional questions? Will the paraprofessional assist with virtual reference? If the paraprofessionals will be referring questions to a professional, are there written guidelines and procedures to ensure consistent referrals and service? Will the employee assist patrons with tasks such as printing, e-mailing, word processing, and photocopying? Will paraprofessionals work at the reference desk only, or will there be other tasks when patrons do not need assistance? In addition to job tasks, there will be questions about other aspects of the job. What will the paraprofessionals' working conditions be? Is it best to have the paraprofessionals work during busy times? Or are they needed for weekends, late night, or evening hours? Will they work with a reference librarian or will they work alone? These questions can be answered by conducting an analysis or assessment. Such an assessment will make the most out of the new position, as well as the training effort. It is important to determine how and when the paraprofessional is needed, and based on those decisions, write the job description and plan training.

There are several approaches to determining what tasks the paraprofessional will be expected to carry out. A good starting point is to have staff analyze what happens at the reference desk over a period of time, and from this analysis, create the list of duties. This method can help determine when the paraprofessional is needed. Another approach is for each member of the reference staff to compile a list of the tasks that he or she believes a paraprofessional should be asked to handle. The department can then meet to review the lists, select the most appropriate tasks, and rank the importance of the tasks.

Tasks should be described as precisely as possible, using active words and avoiding vague phrases like "sometimes" or "could be asked to" (Woodard, 2001). This list can be rewritten into a job description, which will form the basis of the training plan, the job advertisement, and the evaluation form. It is a good idea to incorporate as many reference staff members as possible, since they are stakeholders in this process. Soliciting everyone's input provides the most complete picture of reference activity, and staff will be reassured that the paraprofessional is meant to complement staff, not compete with them (Woodard, 2001). Also, examining reference desk statistics, since they break down reference desk activity into identifiable categories, is helpful (Woodard and Van Der Laan, 1986). If existing categories are too broad or deemed inadequate, institutions with more time can implement another type of measuring system, breaking down the transactions into more discrete categories (directional, equipment requests, ready reference, in-depth research consultation, Internet assistance, etc.) (Barclay, 2004). The paraprofessional's responsibilities can be identified from these categories. It is important to be mindful of the amount of work for a part-time or student employee. How much can a part-time employee realistically learn and do well? In the case of student workers, there may be a high turnover rate. If the library is using part-time employees, it may be in the best interest for service levels to limit the paraprofessionals' tasks and responsibilities but to train them to perform these duties well. It is also important to make sure that there are not

Support staff

1. Answer directional questions and questions appearing on "Frequently Asked Questions" list.
2. Assist patrons with equipment, including printing from computers, making photocopies, and using self-check machine.
3. Respond to questions about Office 2007 and WebCT.
4. Assist with basic services available through library Web page, including finding course reserves and renewals.
5. Perform catalog searches if given an author, book title, or call number.
6. Accompany patrons to the stacks to locate materials.
7. Answer factual questions using "core" reference sources.
8. Get patrons started with databases on "core" source list.

Professional Librarians

1. Perform catalog searches for subjects, keywords, and journal titles, etc.
2. Assist with all research assistance inquiries ("I have to do a paper on," "I have to do research about . . . ," "I have an assignment on . . .").
3. Instruct users in searching noncore databases.
4. Answer factual questions that paraprofessional was unable to answer using "core" sources.
5. Answer any other questions support staff are unable to answer.
6. Assist with above tasks in the absence of support staff.
7. Interpret and explain library services and policies.

Figure 2.1. List of Responsibilities for Support Staff and Professionals

personnel rules that delineate what a paraprofessional can and cannot do; some tasks may fall out of the acceptable range of a job classification.

It can be helpful to create a list that divides tasks and responsibilities between the paraprofessional and the professional librarians. This can provide a clear picture of the role the position will fulfill in the department (see Figure 2.1).

There are also more formal methods of work assessment. While these are beyond the scope of this manual, there are resources that can assist library managers and staff with identifying and collecting information to make informed staffing decisions. The book *Staffing for Results: A Guide to Working Smarter* (Mayo and Goodrich, 2002) covers measuring work, assessing performance, analyzing staff allocation, and reengineering work processes and includes work forms. Similarly, *Managing for Results: Effective Resource Allocation for Public Libraries* (Nelson, Altman, and Mayo, 2000) discusses staff as a resource and provides work forms.

WRITING THE JOB DESCRIPTION

Once the library staff has determined what the paraprofessional will do in the reference department, these tasks can be compiled into a formal job description. A job description lists the duties, responsibilities, required qualifications (e.g., education, skills, experience), and reporting relationships of a particular job. The job description should detail as many of the required tasks as possible.

A written job description can serve as a blueprint for hiring, training, supervising, and evaluating paraprofessionals; lack of a job description will make those tasks more difficult. The training plan should be directly tied to the job description. For example, a paraprofessional who is asked to perform catalog searching will require training in catalog searching. For the supervisor, the job description will help clarify the supervisor's responsibilities and provide criteria for performance evaluation. For the employee, a job description lists the important job functions and helps the employee to understand what is expected (Giesecke and McNeil, 2005).

Libraries have requirements and guidelines for hiring that are related to federal employment and equal opportunity laws. Large libraries may have a human resources officer or department that coordinates hiring. Some public libraries may be subject to city, county, or other municipal guidelines and regulations. College and university libraries may have a central campus human resources office that handles hiring. When writing a job description and hiring employees, supervisors, regardless of the situation, should consult with their human resources or personnel department regarding specific rules, regulations, and guidelines that must be followed in a particular organization. There are also numerous books on how to write a job description, but the first and last authority should be the appropriate human resources department (Giesecke and McNeil, 2005). Following are items that should be considered when writing job descriptions (Goodrich and Singer, 2007). Sample descriptions are given in Figures 2.2, 2.3, and 2.4.

Duties

- Responds to routine and directional questions in person, over the telephone, and via electronic reference service.
- Answers questions using the online catalog and the ready reference collection.
- Assists patrons in using the online catalog, general purpose databases, and ready reference sources.
- Assists patrons in locating materials at library. Directs patrons to the appropriate resources at library.
- Refers involved or in-depth reference questions to the appropriate reference librarian.
- Operates, explains, maintains, and orders supplies for library photocopier, public printers, and self-check machine.
- Other duties as required.

Full-time: Some evening and weekend hours required. Reports to the head of the Information Services Department.

Required skills: Familiarity with computers and other office equipment, such as photocopiers. Familiarity with Internet browsers.

Education: Must have a bachelor's degree.

Salary: $ _____: tuition and health, dental, and vision benefits.

Figure 2.2. Reference Assistant Job Description

Duties

- Under supervision, provide reference and reader's advisory assistance using basic knowledge of both print and electronic resources.
- Assist patrons in use of computers, including OPAC, databases, and Internet, and provide basic PC and printer troubleshooting.
- Under supervision, prepare flyers, brochures, and library displays for purpose of promoting library use.
- Under supervision, assist in developing and maintaining book and other displays.
- Act as person-in-charge in absence of branch manager and librarians.
- Perform related duties as required.

Full-time: Evening and weekend hours required.

Reports to: Branch manager. May function in supervisory capacity as person-in-charge.

Minimum qualifications: Bachelor's degree from an accredited institution.

Salary: $_____/year plus benefits, including tuition reimbursement, health, vision, dental.

Must be a resident of _____. City residency is required on first day of employment.

Figure 2.3. Library Associate Job Description

Duties

- Provides patron assistance with technology and equipment, such as self-check machine, photocopiers, scanners, and computer work stations with software (Microsoft Office, eLearning, Adobe Photoshop) and printing, including paper, toner, and malfunctions.
- Responds to directional and routine questions, both in person and over the telephone, making referrals to librarian when necessary.
- Assists patrons in locating and retrieving materials in the stacks.
- Makes referrals to other campus libraries, departments, and organizations.
- Assists with opening and closing of library.

Part-time, 10–20 hours per week: Must be available to work early mornings, late evenings, and weekends. Students may be required to work alone during those times. During peak times, students may be working with librarians and staff.

Skills and qualifications: Student employees must be undergraduate or graduate students at the university. Must be adept at using WebCT, Adobe Photoshop, and Microsoft Office. Must be familiar with scanning technology, pay–for-print system, and basic computer troubleshooting.

Reports to: Student supervisor.

Salary: $6.55 per hour.

Figure 2.4. Student Assistant Job Description

Job Title: Choose a descriptive, clear title for the position.

Purpose of the Job: This should be a single sentence describing the job, highlighting the most important responsibilities to be performed.

Duties and Responsibilities: List the major duties for which the paraprofessional will be responsible. Tasks should be listed in the order of their importance or by frequency of performance. Do not include procedures for accomplishing the tasks; these should be reserved for the training manual. Usually, positions have between three and seven primary responsibilities. These should be similar enough so that the level of education, experience, and requisite skills is consistent. To provide flexibility for future staffing needs, include the phrase "other duties as required" at the end. This phrase allows for the increase in the position's responsibilities, should the person hired prove to be capable of handling more than the original job description sets forth. Furthermore, changes in the library, such as reorganization or the introduction of new technology, might impact the paraprofessional's responsibilities, requiring a revision of the duties. The phrase "other duties as required" enables libraries to respond to those situations with existing staff.

Reports to: Indicate to whom the paraprofessional reports. This shows all staff members how the position fits into the library's organizational structure. If the person holding the position supervises other employees, that information should be included in this section.

Qualifications: In this section, identify the education, skills, and experience that are needed to do the job, along with those that are desirable to do the job. Federal laws against discriminatory hiring require proof that employment requirements are necessary for the successful completion of the job. Consult a human resources professional or lawyer if there are any questions about the legality of a particular requirement.

Education: Specify the minimum amount of education needed to successfully perform the job. If the position requires a degree, indicate the particular subject specialty required or desired.

Experience: Describe any experience necessary for job performance. The required experience should be relevant for the job. For example, clerical skills should not be required if the employee will never be asked to type or file.

Skills: List any skills required for the job. The job duties may require that paraprofessionals possess software skills, such as Microsoft Office, or can operate equipment such as photocopiers, computers, printers, self-check machines, scanners, etc.

Working Conditions: This section provides information about the library and/or department that could be important to potential applicants. If early morning, evening, or weekend hours are required, state this information. Some indication of the stress level of the job could be provided. For example, note if the reference area is often noisy or fast paced. Indicate whether the position requires physical work, such as shifting books, lifting heavy boxes, or standing for long periods of time.

Salary: Indicate the wage or salary, as well as any benefits for which the paraprofessional will be eligible.

Once the job description has been created, the supervisor will need to make sure that it is approved and/or becomes an official part of a personnel system (Goodrich and Singer, 2007).

PERFORMANCE STANDARDS

Supervisors will also need to determine performance standards for the paraprofessional. Performance standards are "statements that specify or describe work-related behaviors or job outcomes, and that can be evaluated in some objective manner" (Goodson, 1997, p. 11). Individuals will have a better grasp of what the supervisor expects and how to perform if there are standards and a model of performance. There may already be performance standards in place for the reference department, but hiring a new person is a good opportunity to revisit these standards and make adjustments as necessary. Jobs continuously change, and performance standards must reflect what is expected (Goodson, 1997). In addition to the general performance expectations that apply to all staff of the reference department, there may be specifics for the paraprofessional's position. What does the paraprofessional need to know to successfully accomplish the duties in the job description? How should the job be done? How much of the reference collection should the paraprofessional be familiar with? At what point do paraprofessionals refer questions to the professionals? How should the paraprofessional interact with the patron? The questions can be answered by defining competencies, which are defined as knowledge, skills, attitudes, and values required for the successful performance of a job (Cohn and Kelsey, 2005). Competencies for the paraprofessional might include knowledge of certain reference sources, familiarity with the library's collections, and the ability to use appropriate technology (Woodard, 2001). These can be formally incorporated into a competency description, which states the expected behavior of a competent staff member; this statement describes the staff member, not the jobs to be performed (Woodard and Van Der Laan, 1986). This description should:

- describe the correct performance of the job, and
- delineate behaviors. (Woodard, 2001)

These competencies should be developed within individual libraries, in order to match the collections, service models, and user population of that library (Cohn and Kelsey, 2005). Also, competency descriptions are for the staff member, not the jobs to be performed (Woodard and Van Der Laan, 1986). As many staff members as possible should be involved in this process so that there is a clear understanding of service levels.

The standards of performance should be based on things that can be measured, such as knowledge, skills, and behaviors, not attitudes. "Is approachable" is an attitude and therefore subjective. However, the behaviors "Looks up from work," "Asks users if they need assistance," and

"Acknowledges patrons in line" are all actions and can be documented. Knowledge, skills, and behaviors can be expanded and/or modified; attitudes usually cannot (Belcastro, 1998). A suggested basis for a model of performance is the "Guidelines for Behavioral Performance of Reference and Information Service Providers," developed by the Reference and User Services Association Division (RUSA) of the American Library Association. RUSA maintains that "the success of the [reference] transaction is measured not only by the information conveyed, but also by the positive or negative impact of the patron/staff interaction" (RUSA, 2004, p. 14). The development of the behavioral guidelines lists attributes correlated with a perceived positive reference transaction. These guidelines are "intended to be used in the training, development, and/or evaluation of library professionals and staff" (RUSA, 2004, p. 14). A complete copy of the guidelines can be found in the Appendix.

REFERRALS

The referral stage determines and documents when and how paraprofessionals refer users to professional librarians in the department, or in other departments, other libraries, or outside agencies (Woodard, 2001). There are several approaches a library can take.

- The reference staff can examine the questions that patrons ask at the reference desk and determine which can be handled by a paraprofessional. One approach can be to compile those "frequently asked questions" along with the responses (Benefiel, Miller, and Ramirez, 1997). These could be routine questions about library services with very specific answers and/or instructions ("How long can I check out books?" "How can I renew books?" "How much does it cost to photocopy?" "How do I print?" "How can I add money to my print card?", etc.). The paraprofessional would responsible for responding to those questions and requests, referring all other queries to professional librarians.
- The reference department can create a list of "core" resources, both print and electronic, that the paraprofessional must be familiar with (Berkow and Morganstern, 1990). If the question cannot be answered using a source on the list, the staff member would refer the question to a professional librarian. For example, a patron might approach the reference desk looking for a particular statistic. The paraprofessional would consult the statistical sources

on the core list. If the staff member finds the answer, no further action is necessary; otherwise, the paraprofessional would refer the question to a professional.

- The referral can also be task based. Supervisors should carefully examine library tools, such as the catalog and databases, and decide what is appropriate for the support staff and what is too difficult. For example, a library may choose to have support staff search the catalog if given an author, book title, or call number; all other catalog searching would be done by a professional librarian. The paraprofessional might also be trained to search certain databases, such as a "core" list or article databases. Other databases, such as genealogy, citation, or other subject-specific databases would be searched by a professional librarian.

- Referrals can also be time based. Reference staff can agree on a time frame (e.g., five minutes) that should be appropriate for a paraprofessional to answer a question; if the staff member realizes that answering the question will take longer, he or she will know to refer the patron to a professional.

Guidelines for referral may involve one or many of these approaches. Whatever conclusions individual libraries reach about referrals, the plan must ensure that support staff know how and when to refer patrons to professional librarians. Referral procedures must be clear; haphazard procedures are a disservice to patrons (Bracke et al., 2007). The library must also create a culture that supports and rewards referrals to professional librarians, making sure the paraprofessionals understand that it is okay "not to know" and that a referral counts as a "correct answer." This should be stressed in the "Philosophy of Service Memo" (Figure 4.9, Chapter 4). Chapter 8, "Communication Skills," provides more details on how to refer patrons. It is also important that these guidelines be flexible and subject to change. Reference staff should periodically review questions asked at the reference desk, new print and electronic resources, library services, and make changes as necessary. Are there certain categories of questions that the paraprofessional is unable to answer? Also, if the paraprofessional remains in the position for some time, or demonstrates special aptitude for reference service, the types of questions and tasks he or she is permitted to answer could be expanded. Clear guidelines for referral are essential to maintaining a high level of reference service (Benefiel, Miller, and Ramirez, 1997).

Before any kind of concrete planning for training can take place, it is important to have a clear idea of what the paraprofessional will do and to document those tasks in a job description; this will form the basis for the list of training needs. It is also vital to establish how the staff member is expected to perform those tasks. Job tasks and performance standards will form the basis of the training plan and any future performance evaluation for the employee.

REFERENCES

Barclay, Kevin. 2004. "Public Library Reference Desk: Less Is More." *OLA Q* 10, no. 2/3 (Fall): 2–4. Barclay describes how his library analyzed reference statistics and questions to make more efficient use of staff at the reference desk.

Belcastro, Patricia. 1998. *Evaluating Library Staff: A Performance Appraisal System.* Chicago: American Library Association. Belcastro discusses performance standards as they relate to overall quality of service and performance appraisals.

Benefiel, Candace R., Jeannie P. Miller, and Diana Ramirez. 1997. "Baseline Subject Competencies for the Academic Reference Desk." *Reference Services Review* 25, no. 1: 83–93. Describes development of baseline competencies at Texas A&M University's Evans Library. The article mentions the need for these competencies given the use of paraprofessionals at the reference desk and their use in training.

Berkow, Ellen, and Betty Morganstern. 1990. "Getting to the Core: Training Librarians in Basic Reference Tools." *Reference Librarian,* no. 30: 191–206. Describes a project where staff is trained on a core list of reference sources.

Bracke, Marianne Stowell, Michael Brewer, Robyn Huff-Eibl, Daniel R. Lee, Robert Mitchell, and Michael Ray. 2007. "Finding Information in a New Landscape: Developing New Service and Staffing Models for Mediated Information Services." *College & Research Libraries* 68, no. 3 (May): 248–267. Discusses the evaluation of reference service and the resulting implementation of a new staffing model utilizing paraprofessionals.

Cohn, John M., and Ann L. Kelsey. 2005. *Staffing the Modern Library: A How-To-Do-It Manual.* New York: Neal-Schuman Publishers. Chapter 2, "Defining Twenty-first Century Competencies: Determining Standards for the Modern Library," defines competencies and outlines why they are important in libraries.

Giesecke, Joan, and Beth McNeil. 2005. *Fundamentals of Library Supervision.* Chicago: American Library Association. Chapter 8, "Hiring and Interviewing," outlines important issues in creating a job description and its role in the hiring process.

Goodrich, Jeanne, and Paula M. Singer. 2007. *Human Resources for Results: The Right Person for the Right Job.* Chicago: American

Library Association. Goodrich and Singer offer guidance on how managers can use human resources function to support library goals and service priorities. Job descriptions, interviewing and hiring are covered.

Goodson, Carol F. 1997. *The Complete Guide to Performance Standards for Library Personnel.* New York and London: Neal-Schuman Publishers. Provides an explanation of performance standards and tips on how to incorporate these into a library's existing human resources structure. Gives numerous examples of actual performance standards, including paraprofessionals.

Mayo, Diane, and Jeanne Goodrich. 2002. *Staffing for Results: A Guide to Working Smarter.* Chicago and London: American Library Association. This book covers measuring work, assessing performance, analyzing staff allocation, and reengineering work processes and includes work forms.

Nelson, Sandra, Ellen Altman, and Diane Mayo. 2000. *Managing for Results: Effective Resource Allocation for Public Libraries.* Chicago and London: American Library Association. This work discusses staff as a resource and provides work forms to assist with staff allocation.

Reference and User Services Association Division (RUSA). Reference Services Section. Management of Reference Committee. 2004. "Guidelines for Behavioral Performance of Reference and Information Service Providers." *Reference and User Services Quarterly* 44 (Fall): 14–17. The behavioral guidelines for information service providers developed by RUSA cover five areas: approachability, interest, listening/inquiring, searching and follow-up. The text of the guidelines is included in Appendix One.

Woodard, Beth S. 2001. "Reference Service Improvement: Staff Orientation, Training, and Continuing Education." in *Reference and Information Services.* 3rd ed., edited by Richard E. Bopp and Linda C. Smith, 210–244. Englewood, CO: Libraries Unlimited. Woodard's overview of planning for training includes sections covering competencies and job assessment.

Woodard, Beth S., and Sharon J. Van Der Laan. 1986. "Training Preprofessionals for Reference Service." In "Reference Services Today: From Interview to Burnout." *The Reference Librarian* no. 16 (Winter): 233–254. Although the "preprofessionals" are graduate students in library school, Woodard and Van Der Laan's article details the steps in training non-MLS staff for reference work.

3 CREATING A TRAINING PLAN

If paraprofessionals are to provide excellent reference service, the quality of their training is extremely important. To ensure effective training, supervisors must plan, organize, implement, and assess the training. Proper planning will help the library to meet goals, reduce uncertainty for all library staff members, and, in the long run, save time.

A written training plan is helpful for both the new employee and the supervisor. These plans may include checklists, a calendar of activities, a detailed summary of what will be covered, by whom, and with what resources, or a combination of any of these. Planning stages require particular care and time to ensure that paraprofessionals will be taught everything they will need to know for effective job performance. One person or a group can compile the training plan, but to ensure that nothing is omitted, it should be reviewed by several people who were not responsible for its creation and can look with "fresh eyes." Training needs should not be based on memory or supposition; there is the risk that essential content will be omitted from training and/or irrelevant material will be included (Woodard and Van Der Laan, 1986). After a plan has been created, it must be implemented, tested for effectiveness, and revised when necessary. It is worth the time investment to develop an effective training plan; the training process is smoother for all involved persons: trainers, trainees, and supervisors. Training plans help employees by outlining overall expectations, together with the sequence and content of the training. This chapter covers aspects of planning for training: identifying training needs, establishing goals and objectives for a training program, sequencing of training, trainer qualities, choosing training methods, and assembling training materials.

IDENTIFY TRAINING NEEDS

Once the job description is written, a list of training needs can be prepared. What does the paraprofessional need to know to successfully accomplish the duties in the job description? As an example, think about the job description in Figure 2.2. In Figure 3.1, the first duty listed for the reference assistant is to "Respond to routine and directional questions in person, over the telephone, and via electronic reference service." This obviously implies that the paraprofessional will need to know what routine questions are and the proper responses, how to use the telephone, possess knowledge of the library's floor plans and service points, and how to use the software

Task: Responds to routine and directional questions in person, over the telephone, and via electronic reference service.

Needs to know:

Responses to questions that are "routine"
Location of all library service points
Layout of all library floors
How to navigate the library's Web page
How to use online catalog
How to use the telephone properly
Location of phone numbers
How to utilize virtual reference software
Communication techniques
Guidelines and procedures for referrals

Task: Answers questions using the online catalog and the ready reference collection.

Needs to know:

How to use online catalog
How to read a call number
Where circulating and reference materials are housed in building
Communication techniques
What materials are in the ready reference collection
What are the types of ready reference sources (almanacs, dictionaries, etc.)
Guidelines and procedures for referrals
How to use the telephone system

Task: Assists patrons in using the online catalog, general purpose databases, and ready reference sources.

Needs to know:

Where things are in the library
Library circulation policy
Library policy regarding interlibrary loans
Service expectations
Communication techniques
How to use online catalog
How to use general purpose databases
How to use ready reference sources
How to print and e-mail articles
How to read a call number

Figure 3.1. Training Needs List: Reference Assistant

Task: Assists patrons in locating materials at library. Directs patrons to the appropriate resources at library.

Needs to know:

How to use online catalog
How to interpret a catalog record
How to read a call number
Where things are in library
How to place an item on hold or recall
How to request an item from remote storage

Task: Refers involved or in-depth reference questions to the appropriate reference librarian.

Needs to know:

Guidelines and procedures for referrals
Communication techniques
Know who subject specialists are

Task: Operates, explains, maintains, and orders supplies for library photocopier, public printers, and self-check machine.

Needs to know:

Where things are in the building, emphasizing location of supplies and
  equipment
How to use each piece of equipment
How to order supplies
How to troubleshoot each piece of equipment
Whom to call for service for each piece of equipment
How to handle money in each piece of equipment

Figure 3.1 Training Needs List (*Continued*)

---

and technology for electronic reference service. But other training needs are hidden in this task. The paraprofessional will also need to be trained in how to navigate and find answers on the library's Web page, how to use effective communication techniques, and how to refer questions. The following exercise will help generate a list of skills and knowledge that affects the tasks to be done and should be included in the training needs list:

Fill in the blanks:

To do _____, the paraprofessional needs to know _____ or understand_____.

PRIORITIZE TRAINING NEEDS

Once the list of training needs has been assembled, the supervisor will need to decide what the paraprofessional needs to learn first. The paraprofessional cannot learn everything at once, and the supervisor will need to determine what is most important for the efficient running of the department, while maintaining service levels. During the assessment stage (Chapter 2), the department should prioritize tasks. This list will help decide what the paraprofessional should learn first. Another method to help make this decision is to examine the list of training needs and see what "need to know" tasks occur frequently; are there tasks that turn up repeatedly? Also, are there duties that will primarily fall to the paraprofessional such as handling equipment? If so, training in this area should be at the top of the list. A combination of these methods can help determine in what areas the paraprofessional should be trained first.

1. How to use the online catalog (frequently occurs under "needs to know")
2. How to read a call number (intrinsic to helping patrons locate materials)
3. Learn responses to FAQs (a primary use for paraprofessionals)
4. How to navigate the library's Web page (many routine questions can be answered using the Web page and many library services are available via the library home page)
5. How to troubleshoot equipment (another primary duty of paraprofessional)

Once the paraprofessional becomes familiar with these basic tasks and tools, the supervisor can move on to training in other areas, such as database training and virtual reference software training. Other skills, such as communication and understanding how to refer, will be learned on an ongoing basis by observation, training, and coaching.

FORMULATE GOALS AND OBJECTIVES

Once training needs are identified and prioritized, goals and objectives are formulated. Goals broadly describe an activity to be accomplished, while objectives identify each task that must be completed to reach the goal and how that task is completed. A broad training goal might be that, after the completion of the training program, the paraprofessional will be a fully contributing member of the reference staff. Supervisors have a general idea of what the desired outcome of training should be, but it is important that these outcomes, or goals, be documented. Written goals can be given to the paraprofessional and other reference staff members so that expectations are clear to everyone. The employee can then tie the accomplishment of those training goals to successful job performance.

To make the most of written objectives, three components should be present: performance, conditions, and criterion. Performance indicates the task to be accomplished, what the paraprofessional should be able to do. Conditions describe the situation under which performance is to occur, as well as the tools that may be used to complete a task. Criterion is defined as the quality and quantity of work expected and the time allowed to complete the job (Mager, 1975). It is important to make clear what the acceptable performance levels and expected end results should be; these should be covered in the competency description. Objectives must state the action to be carried out and indicate how success will be measured. Each training need tied to the duties in the job description should become a goal for the paraprofessional. The next step is to formulate the objectives, which should identify activities that must be performed to accomplish that training need. For example:

> **Goal:** Paraprofessional will be able to use the online catalog to assist patrons.
>
> **Objective:** Given a catalog record, the paraprofessional will correctly identify all information in the record.

Although this objective consists of one sentence, all three components are present.

- Performance: "identify information in the record" (the task to be accomplished)
- Conditions under which it will be performed: "given a catalog record" (the catalog record is a tool that can be used)
- Criterion: "all information" must be "correctly identified" (the quantity is "all" and the quality is error free)

When considering the objective's performance component, opt for action words that are open to fewer interpretations. Examples include words such as search, write, present, sort, file, etc. Verbs such as know, understand, appreciate, believe, accept, handle, etc., are "fuzzier" and open to more interpretations; these types of words should be avoided (Creth, 1986). It is important to include the behavioral competencies when formulating objectives. When assisting patrons in locating materials, is the paraprofessional expected to accompany the patron to the reference stacks or is providing directions to the stacks an acceptable service level? The instructional objective should indicate the type of service to be provided, so that the trainer can develop training with this in mind.

The second part of an instructional objective is the conditions under which performance occurs; conditions indicate how the task should be completed. There may be some activities that should regularly be conducted from memory, for example, recalling names of prominent authors, identifying general areas within a call number system, or providing directions within the library. Conversely, there may be activities for which paraprofessionals may/should refer to a source. Examples of these activities include consulting written circulation policy when answering questions related to the loan periods, referring to documentation when explaining how to configure a wireless connection in the library, or using a directory when answering certain reference questions. The instructional objectives for training should state whether the paraprofessional may, may not, or must refer to a specific source when doing the activity being learned.

When testing a paraprofessional to determine how well she or he understands a particular activity, it is important that the conditions of testing mirror the instructional objectives (which ideally reflect real life). In other words, after a training session about using a catalog record based on the sample objective above, it would be unfair to require the paraprofessional to explain by heart the pieces of information included in a catalog entry. The objective does not indicate that the paraprofessional must respond to queries about catalog entries from memory; the paraprofessional can and should refer to an actual record.

Finally, the objective should state how success will be measured; this is the criterion. One possible measure of success is speed. Some tasks may need to be completed within a certain time frame. For instance, locating a phone number in a directory should generally take less than three minutes. However, setting time limits may not work for all activities. For example, it is unreasonable for staff to meet an objective requiring them to instruct a patron to use the library's catalog in three minutes. Moreover, it is probably undesirable to indicate to paraprofessionals that patron assistance should be provided according to time factors rather than need.

Another measure of success is accuracy. It is reasonable to expect a paraprofessional to answer a specific percentage of all questions completely and correctly. While it is hard to acknowledge that less than perfect reference service is acceptable, it is important to recognize that no one is perfect, even professional librarians. If the percentage is lower than 100, an attainable goal for the paraprofessional is provided, along with a reasonable guide for evaluating the paraprofessional and the success of training.

Writing down objectives is useful so that colleagues can review them, make suggestions about their importance, and even recommend other topics to be covered. Paraprofessionals can also review the objectives prior to training to get a sense of what they will be expected to learn. Finally, written objectives are useful when training is completed in order to review what was learned. The goal of a training session can be forgotten if the intentions are not considered and recorded. Once the objectives are finalized, the training needs list should be reviewed to account for every task the paraprofessional will perform.

The training content is the difference between the trainee's existing skills and those in the performance expectations and objectives. It is important to remember that paraprofessionals may have varying backgrounds and library experience. They may be unfamiliar with even the most basic reference sources (Woodard and Van Der Laan, 1986). Proceed from the assumption that there is no previous knowledge.

- Teach simple tasks first
- Break down each task to basic components
- Teach only correct procedures
- Keep training cycles short
- Reinforce the training with practice
- Motivate, then reward the trainees
- Repeat until you are sure that your employees understand (Trotta, 2006. p. 81)

After pinpointing areas where training is required but prior to carrying out the training, it can be helpful to use pretests. Administering a pretest can determine what level and amount of training will best prepare the staff person for the job. A pretest can include questions about resources and tools that the paraprofessional will be expected to use. A pretest can also be a demonstration, completion of tasks, or verbal responses (Weaver-Meyers, 2001).

The employee's performance on the pretest will indicate what areas will require coverage and the level of detail; the content of the training modules should be designed to bridge the gap between the employee's existing skill level and the desired level of skills (Woodward and Van Der Laan, 1986). The same pretest can also be repeated after the completion of training to find out how much the paraprofessional has learned. The pretest should be based on the training objectives (Weaver-Meyers, 2001). The supervisor must choose whether to administer a comprehensive pretest that includes everything the employee should know when training is completed or to give a pretest prior to each section of training (e.g., online catalog, call numbers, subject-specific reference sources, etc.).

Using a list of important resources, the supervisor can design questions that will determine what the employee knows about those sources; similarly for tasks, the supervisor can design what the paraprofessional should demonstrate. Another employee should review the test to spot questions and/or tasks that may be too difficult, inappropriate, or irrelevant to the job. For example, knowing the tags of a MARC record is probably not pertinent to the paraprofessional's day-to-day job, but understanding which fields can be used to search for a book in the online catalog is. After the developing the questions, the supervisor should write directions for the pretest, clarifying that the test is only to see where training is needed. Figure 3.2 is provides a sample pretest on the online catalog follows.

After the completion and grading of the pretest, the supervisor should review all of the questions and answers with the employee. It is important

---

DIRECTIONS: This test is designed to indicate how much you already know about the online catalog, and in what areas you will need training. For this reason, do not guess at answers; if you do not know the answer, simply leave that question blank. Some questions may require more than one answer.

True or False

1. If a book title begins with "A, An, or The," you should omit those when looking for the book by its title.
2. You can find journal articles in the online catalog.
3. The call number is what one needs to find the book on the shelf.
4. If you know the author of the book but only part of the title, you can't find the book in the online catalog.
5. If the status of a book is "Not checked out," the book should be on the shelf.
6. If the status of a book is "discharged," the book has been thrown away.

Multiple Choice

1. It is possible to limit a format search by (circle all that apply)
   a. music score
   b. dissertation
   c. DVD
   d. music CD
   e. journal article
2. Which of the following orders can you sort a display by (circle all that apply)
   a. alphabetical
   b. chronological
   c. reverse chronological
   d. relevancy
   e. all of the above

Demonstration Portion

1. Demonstrate how you would find the play *Romeo and Juliet.*
2. How would you find a list of books the library owns that are written by John Grisham?
3. How would you locate a book if a patron handed you a slip of paper containing only the following information:
   PS3515
   .E37
   S8x
4. How would you find a list of books about global warming?
5. How would you find a copy of the short story "Hills Like White Elephants"?

Figure 3.2. Online Catalog Pretest

to identify situations in which the employee has incorrect or incomplete knowledge. Both the library and the paraprofessional will want to avoid a situation where a staff member unwittingly provides incorrect or incomplete information. For example, the staff member might not understand that searching for a copy of a short story or play might involve a more in-depth search than by title alone. If the paraprofessional indicates he or she knows nothing about the steps to locate a short story or play, the supervisor could expect the employee to refer any questions about them to professional librarians. However, if the paraprofessional mistakenly believes he or she understands how to search for plays or short stories, he or she will probably not refer patrons to a professional.

CHOOSE TRAINING METHODS

An important part of planning training is to choose a training method. It is important to use an appropriate method rather than the most convenient one. Choosing a method of training that is most suitable is based on a several considerations. These factors include presence of an experienced trainer, instructional space, available equipment, time and costs of training development, and individual learning styles. However, one of the most important factor is consistency with the training objectives (Woodard, 2001). Some training methods are:

- Lecture: A talk given to present basic ideas and concepts. It is considered to be a less effective method for learning. Lectures should be supplemented by participatory methods, such as a discussion.
- Discussion: An interactive session in which students respond to and talk about a topic.
- Demonstration: Showing the steps to achieve an objective.
- Practice: Learners follow a lecture or demonstration and then follow the steps shown.
- Role-playing: Persons assume roles in a scenario. (Brandt, 2002)

If the learning objective emphasizes knowledge acquisition, such as learning policies, lecture, discussion, and assigned readings are the best methods to use; the supervisor can go over the policies, have the paraprofessional read them, then allow time for the paraprofessional to discuss those policies with the supervisor and ask questions. Some learning objectives involve the acquisition of skills, which are best learned with some sort of practice. The skills of database and catalog searching can be explained via lecture or demonstration, followed by plenty of time for hands-on practice.

While it can be tempting to save time by restricting the training methods to lecture and demonstration only, this is not wise (Woodard, 2001). Research shows that trainees understand concepts better and retain information longer when they are actively involved in the learning process; people learn by doing, not by being told (Piskurich, Beckschi, and Hall, 2000).

When training paraprofessionals about the reference interview, general principles can be communicated by a video or a demonstration, but the staff can practice their skills by role-playing. Role-playing simulates the work environment, providing the paraprofessional a chance to work through real situations and questions and giving the supervisor the opportunity to evaluate and provide feedback (Borin, 2001). This technique also works with learning how to use reference sources. The paraprofessional can be given "real" questions and must then find the source(s) that supply the answer(s). One disadvantage to role-playing is that it is not a favorite of trainees, but does provide a realistic yet nonthreatening situation (Woodard, 2001).

Look at the list of training needs and determine the appropriate methods for training. Use some examples from Figure 3.1:

Training need	**Method for training**
Know library circulation policy	Lecture plus Discussion
Understand library policy regarding interlibrary loan	Lecture plus Discussion
Understand service expectations	Lecture plus Discussion
How to use online catalog	Demonstration plus Practice
How to use databases	Demonstration plus Practice
How to use ready reference sources	Demonstration plus Practice
How to print and e-mail articles	Demonstration plus Practice
How to read a call number	Demonstration plus Practice
Communication techniques	Demonstration plus Role-Playing
Guidelines and procedures for referrals	Lecture/Discussion/Role-Playing

DETERMINE SEQUENCING

Another step in planning is to prioritize and determine the order in which to present the concepts. Sequencing is the efficient ordering of content with the intent of helping the trainee to achieve the objectives (Morrison, Ross, and Kemp, 2004). The training segments should begin with something simple that can serve as a basis for more difficult segments.

There are three general principles behind successful sequencing of training:

1. Proceed from simple to complex.
2. Begin segments with material that the trainees have already learned.
3. Allow trainees time to practice material learned from one segment before proceeding to next segments.

Basic tasks should be explained before more complex tasks are presented, or tasks should be presented in the order that they are to be performed. For example, when teaching a paraprofessional to use an online catalog, begin with author or title searches before progressing to Boolean logic or keyword searches. For a more complete example of tasks for a reference assistant, refer to Figure 2.2. Training related to using the library's online catalog could proceed in this order:

- Discussion of the purpose of the catalog
- Demonstration of different access points for the online catalog
- Explanation that a book can be searched with different pieces of information including title, call number, author, subject
- Demonstration of how to search for titles in the catalog
- Discussion of how author's names are entered (last name, first name)
- Demonstration of how to search for authors in the catalog
- Discussion of call numbers and their purpose
- Demonstration of how to search by call number
- Discussion of subject headings and controlled vocabulary
- Explanation of cross-references
- Demonstration of subject searching

In this sequence, the first step is for the paraprofessional to become familiar with searching for titles. Generally, title searches are straightforward and will not involve cross-references. This eases the paraprofessional into searching the catalog and allows him or her to gain familiarity with screen displays. The next step is to search by call number. The searching by call number is also straightforward, but the paraprofessional will need to understand the purpose of call numbers and what they mean. The next segment is author searching, which may involve cross-references. Finally, the paraprofessional moves to subject searching, which can get quite complex with cross-references, and broader and narrower topics. By learning subject searching last, the paraprofessional should be somewhat familiar with the catalog, including the presentation of information and functionality, so that the focus can be learning the concept of subject headings. Thus, the training progressed from the simple task of learning the catalog well enough to complete title searches to a more complex understanding of cross-references to the most complex task—complete subject searches (McDaniel and Ohles, 1993).

SELECT TRAINING MATERIALS

Along with training methods, training materials should be selected. The materials should complement the training method and support the training needs.

POLICY AND PROCEDURE MANUAL

A core for the training material should be the reference department's policy and procedure manual. Policy and procedure manuals serve as

- a place where all related policies and procedures are located;
- a tool to ensure uniformity in staff actions and consistent service; and
- a guide to making decisions together with a record of past decisions. (Stueart and Moran, 2002)

In the case of a reference department, policies and procedures should set forth guidelines for providing reference services in order to ensure a uniform standard of service of the highest quality. These policies and procedures should

- establish standards of service;
- offer guidelines for levels and limits of service;
- help resolve conflicts, such as why library staff do not put more than ten books on hold or why a staff member cannot spend more than a certain amount of time answering a telephone reference question; and
- establish priorities in the hierarchy of services. (Katz, 2002)

Including a policies and procedures manual in the training materials will facilitate quick orientation of new employees by providing them with a basic understanding of the department and its activities. In addition, manuals can reinforce the contents of the training sessions, place responsibility for learning the basic contents of the manual on the employee, indicate desired levels of performance, and provide a written reference to policies, procedures, and basic job skills for employees. If the library does not have a policies and procedures manual for the reference department, developing one is well worth the time investment.

"How to" develop a policy manual is beyond the scope of this book, but the following issues need to be taken into account:

- Who is going to develop the manual? Will it be a committee or task force, a supervisor with staff input, or the supervisor alone?

- What will be included in the manual? Memos, e-mails, reports, notes, departmental documents, existing policy statements, etc.,will all need to be gathered, reviewed, and possibly adapted for the manual.

- How will the manual be evaluated and revised? Manuals must be both effective and up to date.

Many libraries now have their policy and procedures manual online. Online manuals can take the form of an intranet or an internal wiki (collection of Web pages designed to enable anyone who accesses it to contribute or modify content). The advantage to having a manual online is that the contents can be hyperlinked. There may also be valuable tips (database or catalog searching, assignment alerts, etc.) contained on staff blogs or listservs. Important and useful information might be disseminated in many forms. Make sure the paraprofessional understands all the places that policies, procedures, tips, etc., can be located.

If there is not a policies and procedures manual in place, and there is insufficient time to compile one, staff should take the time to identify key policies and to document important procedures for the training materials. It is helpful to define the difference between policy and procedure so that the concepts are clear. Policies generally provide guidelines that employees can follow in their work such as: The reference staff strives to provide accurate information and materials in response to requests from library patrons in an efficient, courteous, and timely manner. To be effective, a policy needs to be comprehensive enough to address the implementation of the service offered but simple enough to be understood and remembered by staff members (Burgett, 2006).

Reviewing policies from other libraries can provide ideas on what to include and how to word the policy. It is important to remember that while other institutions' policies will have useful elements, it is best to model a

> "Policies and regulations are intended to ensure that the library operates in ways that are consistent with the organization's mission, goals, and objectives—doing the right things. Procedures and guidelines, on the other hand are much more concerned with efficiency—doing those things right" (Nelson and Garcia, 2003, p. 3).

policy on that of a "peer" institution with a similar mission and services. For example, a medical library will have a different policy toward medical reference than a public library. Each reference department will need to tailor the materials to suit its own needs.

Procedures go through specific tasks step by step. They describe how an activity is performed, who is to perform the activity (when appropriate), and the chronology of the steps taken.

When compiling the policies for the training materials, include information that affects reference desk service in the policy statements, such as:

- Circulation of reference materials
- Internet use
- Statement of confidentiality regarding patron inquiries
- Amount of time spent answering questions for all types of reference service
- Special statements regarding financial, medical, and legal reference
- Printing, faxing, photocopying for patrons
- Homework assistance (Larson and Totten, 1998)

There may be policies from other departments that impact reference service. For example, if the reference desk fields numerous questions about locating textbooks and the library does not collect textbooks, it is wise to include the library's collection development policy on textbooks in the training materials. If the list of training needs makes mention of specific policies, those policies should be included in the training materials. For example, the list of training needs in Figure 3.1 includes knowing library circulation policy and understanding library policy regarding interlibrary loans. Therefore, training materials will need to include the policies for circulation and interlibrary loans. If the list of training needs includes items that involve following procedures, those should be included in the training materials. Based on the list of training needs, procedures should be included for items such as:

- Adding paper or toner to photocopiers
- Clearing jams from printers and photocopiers
- Using the self-check machine
- Using the photocopier
- Handling cash
- Rebooting computers
- Placing an item on hold or recall

- Requesting an item from remote storage
- Using the telephone system
- Downloading information from electronic resources
- Ordering supplies
- Adding paper to self-check machine

Gear the language of the procedures to its readers. Simplify the steps as much as possible so that staff can easily follow them. It can be useful to think, "If no reference staff member is present, what would a paraprofessional employee need to know to smoothly run the library?"

GLOSSARY

A glossary should be included with the training materials. Libraries are full of acronyms and jargon, most of which will be unfamiliar to the paraprofessional. Providing a glossary of library terms (which includes acronyms and abbreviations) will help the new employee learn the language of libraries. If such a document does not exist, it can be worth the time to develop one. The supervisor can compile a core list of glossary entries and solicit input from staff members. Are there any terms that should be added or deleted? It is important to develop the glossary for an employee with little or no library experience and not to include too many entries. The glossary should be kept generic, retaining only those terms that all library staff should be familiar with. As with any training document, it will be necessary to review and possibly revise the glossary (Davis, 1994). Refer to the Glossary at the end of this book as an example.

OTHER IDEAS FOR TRAINING MATERIALS

For catalog and database training, vendor-supplied materials can be invaluable in training. The library should contact catalog, database, and equipment vendors to see if there are interactive tutorials available to include as part of training; many online resources have tutorials included as part of the product. In addition, library associations, other libraries, or state libraries may have training material available for use; a simple search on the Internet may yield good results. The supervisor will need to decide if the material from other organizations is appropriate for a particular library; the initial time saved by using content developed at another organization may not be worth it if the materials are unsuitable, resulting in poor work or the need to retrain. Other training materials to include could be locally developed tip sheets on core databases, basic search tips on using the catalog, and instructions on how to read call numbers. If tip sheets are incorporated from larger manuals, reference the manuals in case there are questions that the tip sheets do not include.

MODULES AND CHECKLISTS

The supervisor must teach the employee on the use of reference sources, as well as other tools and skills necessary to help patrons locate information. The supervisor should create a list of all of the resources and tools the paraprofessional should know how to use at the completion of training. Obvious resources include the online catalog, reference books, core databases, and the Internet, but there are also tools such as federated search solutions and linking software that libraries have implemented to streamline the process of information retrieval. After selection, the sources and tools should be ranked by importance as to what should be covered first.

In order to teach the paraprofessional how to use resources in the manner best suited for the library, the reference department should consider creating its own training materials. One type of training material the department can create is a checklist. Checklists are designed for tasks, services, and resources that may be very specific to individual libraries; examples include online catalogs, self-service points available through a library's Web site, etc. Training checklists enumerate what must be covered so that the paraprofessional thoroughly understands how to perform a particular task or understand a resource. In order to design a checklist, the supervisor should perform a task, dissect it into components, and explain each section. Similarly, for a resource, such as an online catalog or database, the supervisor should examine that resource and list everything the staff member needs to know about that resource, such as search fields, display and sort options, etc.

Other forms of training materials are modules providing information which will help the staff member understand resources (reference sources, call numbers, etc.) along with practice questions/exercises and answers. These modules can be prepared for specific sources and subject areas. One method to design modules is to select a group of resources with which the paraprofessional must be familiar and construct practice questions that can be answered using these sources. Modules are helpful because supervisors are forced to consider important sources in a thoughtful, structured manner. Without the modules, there may be a tendency to haphazardly acquaint the staff member with important resources by pointing to resources and saying, "This source is good for X; this source is good for Y." Modules permit the employee to study and/or practice using important sources, while at the same time, supplying the paraprofessional specific information about the resources for future referral. Modules can also include sample pages from the sources or copies of handouts that are given to patrons.

CHECKLISTS FOR DESIGNING MODULES

General considerations for designing modules:

- The supervisor, in consultation with other staff members, should identify commonly asked questions and/or the most often used sources; the training modules should emphasize the resources and tools most frequently used by reference staff.
- Describe and explain the differences between the sources. Emphasize that not all sources are alike, even if they cover the same subject areas. Otherwise the paraprofessional runs the risk of gravitating to the same source to answer questions.
- When possible, reference staff should identify subject areas (e.g., business, statistics, government, etc.) so that the supervisor can prepare training modules for these categories.
- Design the questions to highlight the differences among the sources but also to reflect questions that patrons ask.
- Describe the purpose of the source and offer examples of when the source can be used.

Considerations for print resources:

- How is the source arranged? Is the arrangement alphabetical or by subject? Is the work divided into sections?
- Is there introductory material that is helpful?
- What types of indexes are available? What are the differences?

Considerations for electronic resources:

- What are the differences between a basic search and advanced search? Is it better to always use a certain type of search? Is it possible to restrict a search to a subset of an electronic resource (e.g., images only)? Are browse features available?
- Can the content be browsed? Is there an electronic index?
- What are the fields that allow one to retrieve information? (e.g., many business databases can be searched by company name, ticker symbol, etc.).
- Electronic resources often have extra features; examples include dictionaries, thesauri, timelines, atlases, links to

news stories, recommended Web sites, etc. What are these features and how can they be accessed?

- What options are there to print, download, export, and save information?
- How do the search results display?

Chapters 5, 6, and 7 offer examples of training checklists and modules. Chapter 5 is meant to cover basic skills, things the paraprofessional should be taught right away. Chapter 6 presents more advanced skills. Chapter 7 presents ready-reference skills in different modules: encyclopedias, government information, statistics, health and medicine, international information. These are intended as samples to help prepare handouts to be used for training paraprofessionals in individual libraries. Because the world of databases changes so rapidly, there are no modules for individual databases; the database module is meant to cover the basics that can be adapted and tailored for specific databases. Each library will need to decide what sources, skills, and tools the paraprofessional will need to learn in order to provide effective reference service. Some libraries may still rely heavily on print; others, strictly on electronic resources. Some libraries may need to train in resources that are not considered "standard" reference sources. For example, a library that gets many requests for assistance with citations may train the paraprofessional with basic use of various style manuals. If the paraprofessional will be responsible for assisting children and young adults, it may be wise to compile training modules for known assignments and projects. These can include local history projects, science fair projects, assignments for Black History Month and other heritage months, holidays, etc. If the community or university is associated with a famous person (actress, architect, football coach, etc.), there may be resources compiled to answer those types of questions.

When all of the sources in a given training module have been reviewed, the paraprofessional should have time to answer the practice questions and check his or her responses against the prepared answers. The trainer should be available to answer questions and review any sources as needed. For tasks where checklists are utilized, the trainer should go over each step with the paraprofessional.

Basic Adult Learning Principles

- Adults bring experience to the learning situation
- Adults prefer variety
- Adults want to learn
- Adults learn best by doing
- Treat adults as adults
- Ensure practicality of training (Piskurich, Beckschi, and Hall, 2000, p. 126)

THE TRAINER

The library will need to decide who will train the paraprofessional. It may be the supervisor, but some training may fall to other individuals. Trainers are the key to successful learning. If the trainer displays poor characteristics, much of the work put into the training process will be undone, even with a well-thought-out training plan. While the trainer should be knowledgeable about any subjects he or she will train on, the trainer may not be the employee with the most knowledge if the other abilities are lacking. An employee who possesses the most knowledge but also has a poor attitude toward the library is not a desirable trainer. In this situation, a supervisor could end up with a trained employee with a poor attitude. If persons other than the supervisor will be training, these persons should be apprised of expectations of training and lists of duties. Training paraprofessionals takes a great deal of time, and the librarian assigned to the task may need to give up some other duties during the design and implementation of the training program; the library must be prepared to commit the personnel, time, and resources to the project. In addition, supervisors should work with trainers to ensure that the content and process of training are meeting the needs of the department or library. Even if there is little choice about who is to do the training, there are several things to keep in mind (Creth, 1986). Persons training should possess the following qualities:

- Be able to demonstrate enthusiasm about what is being taught.
- Be extremely knowledgeable about the subjects that they are teaching.
- Be able to model desired behaviors.
- Be committed to reaching the goals of a training program.
- Be able to use appropriate instruction methods.

> **Desirable Trainer Qualities**
>
> - Subject expertise
> - Training skills
> - Ability to relate theory to practice
> - Self-confidence
> - Ability to instill confidence in users
> - Supportive of adult learners
> - Skill at establishing a supportive climate
> - Commitment to helping others learn
> - Competence in using relevant training methods
> - Credibility with participants (Allan, 2003, p. 42; Scott, 2001, pp. 116–117)

Ideally, those who train should possess several personal attributes in addition to those listed above. These include openness to and respect for different people and learning styles/paces, flexibility, enthusiasm for working with people, ability to tie training content to learner needs, and talent for judging employees' work performance, organizational skills, and a positive commitment to the training, library, and to library work.

Planning is an essential piece of the training process. Taking the time to plan each aspect of training will help to ensure a thoughtful, well-developed training program. It is important to include as many reference staff members as possible at each stage of planning. Careful planning will benefit the supervisor and trainer, the paraprofessionals, the reference department, and, ultimately, the library as a whole.

REFERENCES

Allan, Barbara. (Moran, Barbara, North American editor). 2003. *Training Skills for Library Staff* Lanham, MD. Scarecrow Press. Presents ideas, tools, and techniques for training, and is geared toward both new and experienced library trainers.

Borin, Jacqueline. 2001 "Training, Supervising, and Evaluating Student Information Assistants." *The Reference Librarian* no. 72: 195–206. In the context of using student assistants to provide reference service, Borin discusses the use of role-playing in training those workers when to refer questions to professional librarians.

Brandt, D. Scott. 2002. *Teaching Technology: A How-To-Do-It Manual for Librarians*. New York: Neal-Schuman. In his manual on how to teach technology, Brandt describes some instructional design procedures, including various methods of instruction.

Burgett, Shelly Wood. 2006. "If It Isn't Written, It Doesn't Exist: Creating a Library Policy Manual." In *It's All About Student Learning: Managing Community and Other Libraries in the 21st Century*, edited by David R. Dowell and Gerard B. McCabe, 253–260. Westport, CT: Libraries Unlimited. This chapter provides a step-by-step guide to the "never ending process" of developing a library policy manual.

Creth, Shelia D. 1986. *Effective On-the-Job Training*. Chicago and London: American Library Association. Written for libraries, this slender volume provides an overview of the process, needs, planning, implementation, and evaluation of training.

Davis, H. Scott. 1994. *New Employee Orientation: A How-To-Do-It-Manual for Librarians*. New York: Neal-Schuman Publishers. Although devoted entirely to orientation, Davis has information useful for planning of training, especially his rationale behind providing a glossary.

Katz, William A. 2002. *Introduction to Reference Work: Volume Two: Reference Services and Reference Processes*. 8th ed. New York: McGraw Hill. In the chapter "Reference Service Policies and Evaluation" William Katz presents the purpose of policies and procedures specifically for reference departments.

Larson, Jeanette, and Hermann L. Totten. 1998. *Model Policies for Small and Medium Public Libraries*. New York: Neal-Schuman Publishers. Discusses polices and instructions on how to develop them. Especially helpful are the chapters with sample policies; Chapter 8 is devoted to "Reference and Information Services."

Mager, Robert F. 1975. *Preparing Instructional Objectives*, 2nd ed. Belmont, CA: Fearon Publishers. As the title indicates, this work describes how to formulate objectives and offers guided practice in doing so.

McDaniel, Julie Ann, and Judith K. Ohles. 1993. *Training Paraprofessionals for Reference Service: A How-To-Do-It Manual for Librarians*. New York: Neal-Schuman. This work, the preceding edition to this one, still provides a solid foundation for planning of training.

Morrison, Gary R., Steven M. Ross, and Jerrold E. Kemp. 2004. *Designing Effective Instruction*. 4th ed. Hoboken, NJ: John Wiley. This textbook provides an excellent overview of instructional design.

Nelson, Sandra, and June Garcia. 2003. *Creating Policies for Results: From Chaos to Clarity*. Chicago, American Library Association. Another book in the "for Results" series, this one is a comprehensive guide to creating library policies.

Piskurich, George M., Peter Beckschi, and Brandon Hall, editors. 2000. *The ASTD Handbook of Training Design and Delivery: A Comprehensive Guide to Creating and Delivering Training Programs, Instructor-led, Computer-based, or Self-directed.* New York: McGraw-Hill Professional.

Scott, Wendy L. 2001. "How to Develop Training Skills." In *Staff Development: A Practical Guide,* edited by Elizabeth Fuseler Avery, Terry Dahlin, and Deborah A. Carver, 116–117. Chicago: American Library Association.

Stueart, Robert D., and Barbara B. Moran. 2002. *Library and Information Center Management*. 6th ed. Greenwood Village, Colorado: Libraries Unlimited. Chapter 3, "Planning Information Services," contains a section on policy making.

Trotta, Marcia. 2006. *Supervising Staff: A How-To-Do-It Manual for Librarians*. New York: Neal-Schuman Publishers. Chapter 4, "Directing Ongoing Staff Training," gives guidance to supervisors on determining training needs, setting goals, and conducting training.

Weaver-Meyers, Pat. L. 2001. "Creating Effective Training Programs." In *Staff Development: A Practical Guide*, 3rd ed., edited by Elizabeth Fuseler Avery, Terry Dahlin, and Deborah A. Carver, 125–128. Chicago and London: American Library Association. Weaver-Meyers succinctly presents the steps to create a training program, from needs analysis to program evaluation.

Woodard, Beth S. 2001. "Reference Service Improvement: Staff Orientation, Training, and Continuing Education." In *Reference and Information Services,* 3rd ed., edited by Richard E. Bopp and Linda C. Smith, 210–244. Englewood, CO: Libraries Unlimited. Woodard's overview of planning for training includes sections covering competencies, assessment, training objectives, and methods.

Woodard, Beth S., and Sharon J. Van Der Laan. 1986. "Training Preprofessionals for Reference Service." In "Reference Services Today: From Interview to Burnout." *The Reference Librarian* no. 16 (Winter): 233–254. Although the "preprofessionals" are graduate students in library school, Woodard and Van Der Laan's article details the steps in training non-MLS staff for reference work.

4 ORIENTATION

Staff orientation is "an initial training process designed to acquaint new employees with various aspects of the organization, including established goals, policies, and procedure; the physical environment; other personnel and working relationships, job duties and responsibilities; and fringe benefits" (Young, 1983, p. 214).

As with any new employee, the paraprofessional needs to be oriented to not only the library but to the reference department before actual training in job tasks begins. Employee orientation serves to welcome the new staff member, provides information about the organization and the work, and builds a solid foundation for future training. During orientation, the supervisor will answer the "who," "what," "where," "when," "how," and "why" of the library, the department, and the position. Successful orientation will:

- decrease employee turnover;
- enable the staff member to be productive as soon as possible;
- create feelings of satisfaction and enthusiasm in the paraprofessional; and
- allow an employee to quickly feel like a part of the department. (Woodard, 2001)

This chapter covers the various aspects of orientation including planning, initial preparation, the "housekeeping" duties necessary with any new employee, orientation sessions, and departmental introductions.

PLANNING ORIENTATION

Most organizations have some sort of orientation for any new employee in place. Some organizations (universities, municipalities, etc.) may have formal orientation sessions that all employees attend which cover the things that pertain to the entire organization such as various types of insurance, retirement plans, important policies, and legal issues. Smaller organizations may have smaller orientations where a human resources officer (or designated person) will cover things such as filling out necessary forms, tax withholding, paydays, various payroll deductions, such as taxes and retirement plans, number and length of breaks, holidays, sick time, vacation time, overtime, dress codes, time recording procedures, etc. This does not preclude the necessity of an orientation to the reference department and the library.

To assist in planning the paraprofessional's orientation to the reference department, it can be helpful to distinguish between orientation and training. Orientation enables employees to find out how they fit into the total organizational structure of the library; training provides employees instruction on how to complete specific job tasks (Rubin, 1991). Information imparted during orientation tends to be organization-specific and is generally not applicable elsewhere (Woodard, 2001). However, the two are closely related, and it may be difficult to see where orientation ends and training begins.

With these definitions in mind, the supervisor should consider what the paraprofessional needs to know before, and soon after, he or she starts employment. The supervisor should try not to have too much overlap with topics that would be covered by another orientation session, and should work to coordinate with the individual responsible for handling general orientation to see who handles what. Some things, such as payroll and tax withholding may be obvious, but other things, such as who handles the paperwork to register for an e-mail account or who explains the organization chart, are not.

In addition, the supervisor will need to explain how some personnel matters translate to the reference department. For example, the human resources officer (or designated individual) would explain the number of sick and vacation days, but the supervisor would need to discuss the department policies and procedures for contacting the department in case of illness and how vacation days are scheduled in the reference department. The supervisor would also discuss how time off for other employees might affect the paraprofessional's schedule (e.g., if the student workers do not show up, the paraprofessional may be responsible for working more hours at the desk) (DiMarco, 2005).

An orientation checklist is recommended ("Checklist for New Employee Orientation," 2000). This list should be as complete as possible to ensure that nothing the paraprofessional needs is omitted. A checklist will also assist in keeping track of what orientation tasks have been accomplished and what remains. This checklist can be arranged topically or chronologically. Each institution will need to decide what its new employee will need and what can be accomplished within a certain time frame. A timetable should be sketched out so that the employee will know what to expect during the first few weeks and so that other staff members involved in the orientation can arrange their schedules as needed. The plan must allow time for the employee to absorb and reflect on the information presented, and to ask questions. The time table should also be flexible, as the paraprofessional may progress more quickly in some areas and require more time in others (Weingart, Kochan, and Hedrich, 1998).

To ensure a smoother transition, consider providing the paraprofessional with the following items prior to arrival:

- Welcome letter
- Temporary parking pass
- A copy of the first week's agenda
- Directions to the campus/library
- Points of interest near the library (restaurants, ATMs, etc.)
- Contact information for any questions (DiMarco, 2005, p. 111)

Sample checklists are provided in Figure 4.1 and Figure 4.2. When compiling the checklist, it can be helpful to think, "What does the parapro-fessional need to know to understand the work environment, culture, values, etc., of this library and the reference department? What information will make the transition less stressful? What preparations can be made to assist in this process?"

Part I: Prior to First Day

_____ Prepare letter of welcome and orientation packet.

_____ Notify department staff and other appropriate persons of beginning date.

_____ Develop training program plan and assemble materials.

_____ Assign orientation responsibilities to other staff members if appropriate.

_____ Arrange for preparation of employee's PC.

_____ Arrange for e-mail account.

_____ Check employee work area for necessary supplies/equipment and order if needed.

Part II: First Day (may overlap with first week, as time allows)

_____ Escort new employee to human resources for paperwork (I-9 form, tax forms, benefits).

_____ Show employee work space.

_____ Introduce to reference department staff.

_____ Provide employee with keys and security code for front door.

_____ Give employee orientation package and explain contents.

_____ Work area tour, including:

• major entrances and exits

• restrooms

• vending machines

• staff lounge

_____ Take employee to lunch.

_____ Provide unscheduled time for review of orientation materials, arrange office area, and set up voicemail.

Part III: First Week (may overlap with first day, as time allows)

_____ Have employee register for e-mail account.

_____ Provide information on library intranet and how to register for ap-propriate library staff listservs.

Figure 4.1. Sequence-Based Checklist

_____ Discuss basic rules and regulations, including:

- work schedule
- lunch and breaks
- procedure for calling in
- location of Personnel Policy Manual
  other pertinent policies (e.g., use of telephone for personal calls, dress code)
  answer other questions

_____ Review security, safety, and emergency procedures. Point out location of disaster manual in department and on intranet.

_____ Provide copy of job description and discuss position:

- explain importance of the position and how it relates to other positions in the team and the library
- discuss probationary period and evaluation criteria
- discuss annual evaluation and evaluation criteria
- explain team structure and departmental structure
- explain regular departmental meetings
- review training plan

_____ Show where supplies are located and how to order supplies.

_____ Review instructions for equipment.

- photocopier
- telephone
- fax machine

_____ Tour library and introduce library staff.

_____ Provide overview of library home page.

_____ Discuss philosophy of reference service.

_____ Departmental introductions, as appropriate.

Part IV: Second Week

_____ Continue to work with employee describing his/her duties and seeking and answering questions.

_____ Discuss training plans.

_____ Discuss standards and other criteria for performance evaluations.

_____ Departmental introductions, as appropriate.

Part V: Third Week

_____ Continue to meet regularly with the employee to train, monitor, and provide feedback to the employee on progress.

Figure 4.1. Sequence-Based Checklist (*Continued*)

Basics
- Department tour
- Department policies
- Office keys
- Computer setup
- E-mail setup

Building
- Library tour
- Emergency procedures
- Opening and closing procedures
- After-hours access

Equipment and Supplies
- Mail procedures
- Telephone use
- Ordering office supplies
- Location and use of photocopier
- Location and use of fax machine

Work Schedule
- Work hours
- Lunch and breaks
- Scheduling vacation time
- Notification when ill or tardy

Job Responsibilities
- Review of job description
- Standards and expectations
- Probationary and annual review criteria and procedures
- Departmental overview
- Strategic Plan and Mission of Library as related to department

Figure 4.2. Subject-Based Checklist

PREPARATION

The implementation of orientation begins between hiring the new paraprofessional and his or her first day of work. A welcoming letter, such as that found in Figure 4.3, should be sent to indicate the starting date; where, to whom, and at what time he or she should report; and any forms or documents he or she should bring (e.g., birth certificate, social security card, driver's license, etc.), if appropriate. In addition, the letter could indicate what the paraprofessional can expect for the first few weeks, what work will be like at the beginning, and the aspects of orientation. The supervisor could also call the new paraprofessional several days before the starting date to confirm the first week's schedule and answer any last-minute questions.

At the library, certain preparations should be made for the new employee's arrival:

- The paraprofessional's work space should be set up. The area should be clean and stocked with files relevant to the position, supplies, a computer, a telephone. Key reference materials should also be on hand, such as a telephone directory, the departmental policy and procedure manual, a personnel manual, etc. (DiMarco, 2005).

- Take care of details such as keys or key request forms, preparing the identification process, setting up computer and e-mail accounts. If it is not possible to have everything ready and available on the first day, do as much as possible to facilitate speedy accomplishment of this "housekeeping." Having keys, a proper ID, computer, and e-mail accounts as quickly as possible makes a new hire feel welcome and part of the organization (DiMarco, 2005).

- Plan the tour of the department (DiMarco, 2005).

- Begin thinking about other departments that the paraprofessional should visit and contact those departments as necessary (DiMarco, 2005).

- Inform other staff members about new paraprofessional, including starting date, background (e.g., former jobs, education), and the job description.

- Assemble the "Orientation Packet." This packet consists of materials given to the employee on his or her first day. The orientation packet's contents will probably not be everything the employee will receive during orientation, but it should contain materials deemed to be "core" to any new library position. Each institution will have its own idea of what is core; Figure 4.4 has examples of what could be included (Davis, 1994).

Tips in developing an orientation plan:

- Be specific when providing information in the plan. Do not assume anything.
- Communicate plan to all library employees and other appropriate offices. This is the opportunity to fix potential problems.
- Write down every aspect of the plan.
- Use checklists whenever possible. (DiMarco, 2005, p. 110)

Sample 1

Dear _____

I am pleased to welcome you to the staff of _____ Library. As we discussed, you will be working as a part-time library associate, twenty hours per week at the rate of $XX.XX per hour.

Mr. O'Shea, Head of Reference Services, will expect to meet you at the reference desk at 9:00 a.m. on Monday, July 2.

If I can be of any further assistance to you, please feel free to contact me at XXX-XXXX. I look forward to working with you.

Sincerely,

Director

Sample 2

Dear _____

I am very glad that you will be joining the Reference Department staff. Because I am your immediate supervisor, we will be working closely together. I look forward to getting to know you and developing a mutually rewarding work relationship. Your first few weeks here are likely to be hectic ones. I will try to reduce any uncertainty you may feel by letting you know what to expect during your first days and weeks here.

I will meet you at 9:00 a.m. at the main reference desk. The first few hours of the day will be devoted to paperwork in our Human Resources Department. After that, I will show you your work space, take you around the department, and introduce you to your coworkers. I will also be taking you to lunch on your first day. You will receive an orientation packet, which I will go over with you. The first day of a new job can be exhausting, so I will be providing you with some down time to review the materials in the packet, set up your office area, your voice mail, and get your bearings.

The orientation packet will contain a copy of the Reference Department Policy Manual. During the first week, you will have time to read the manual. You and I will meet during the first week to discuss the manual and to provide you with an opportunity to ask questions.

During the first week, we will also begin to discuss your job and go over other "housekeeping" issues, such as calling in sick and lunch breaks. You will also get a library tour and have more in-depth visits with other library departments.

Beginning your second week of work, we will review the training plan and begin training. We will have you "shadow" at the desk. We ask that you not try to answer any questions, but simply observe the librarian you are working with. This is an important part of your training.

During the third week, when you are scheduled at the reference desk, we ask that you start to answer directional questions, but continue to observe librarians as they answer more in-depth reference questions. By the fourth week, you may begin answering any questions with which you feel comfortable.

Again, I am looking forward to working with you. Please feel free to contact me with any questions or concerns, XXX-XXXX.

Respectfully yours,

Immediate Supervisor

Figure 4.3. New Employee Welcome Letters

- Library Organization Chart
- Library Calendar
- Information on History of the Library
- Copy of Library Newsletter
- Library Floor Plans
- Relevant Maps (campus, neighborhood, etc.)
- Policies and Procedures Manual
- Telephone/E-mail List
- Library Hours
- Pay-Day Schedule
- Orientation Schedule

Figure 4.4. Orientation Packet Checklist

FIRST DAYS

The first few days of an employee's new job are crucial. Not only will the supervisor need to impart a great deal of essential information, but he or she will also need to make the new employee feel comfortable. The first few hours on the job should be devoted to welcoming the new employee into the department and taking care of necessary personnel procedures. The next few days will involve the paraprofessional learning about the overall structure and organization of the library and department, as well as about basic day-to-day operations.

The paraprofessional should have a copy of the library organization chart; the supervisor or a personnel officer can review the structure and organization of the library. It is also important for the paraprofessional to learn how the library fits in at the university, college, or community in which it is situated. If the library has a strategic plan, the supervisor should provide the paraprofessional with a copy so that he or she can see what direction the library is taking and why.

One area that is critical to the orientation process is discussion of emergency and security procedures; this is especially important for a public service position. The supervisor should review what steps to take in various situations: threats, fire, suspicious behavior, medical emergencies, power outages, hazardous weather, etc. The paraprofessional should also have up-to-date copies of the procedures that must be followed and know where an emergency or disaster manual is kept. The employee should be able to locate all emergency exits and alarms. Also, the paraprofessional should know how to respond when the alarms are set off by careless patrons (Weingart, 1998).

Employers everywhere are grappling with employee's use of social software, such as personal blogs and My-Space and Facebook pages. It is important to discuss with paraprofessionals how the organization views such activities. For example, it may be humorous to describe a bad day at the reference desk in a personal blog but this may be inappropriate, not to mention a violation of patron privacy. Make sure the paraprofessional understands the boundaries and the rules. If the paraprofessional enjoys social software, consider having him or her play a prominent role in creating or contributing to a blog, MySpace and/or Facebook profile, or Flickr photo page for the library.

REFERENCE DEPARTMENT AND DESK

The paraprofessional will need both an immediate tour, as well as a more in-depth explanation of the reference department. This will include coworker introductions, a tour of the office, location of break rooms and snack and drink machines, bathrooms, and supplies. More in-depth information should include job responsibilities of each staff member, how to obtain supplies, reference desk schedules, and explanation of department items (see Figure 4.5). It can be helpful to provide the paraprofessional with information on what happens during a typical year in the reference department. This helps to the paraprofessional to get into the "flow" of the department. If available, departmental meeting minutes give a sense of the department's "history" and what issues the department is facing. This is also the time to review the new paraprofessional's job description, answer any job-specific questions, and emphasize important aspects of the job. The paraprofessional will need to understand the responsibilities of the new position how the position fits into the department and why he or she was hired. If the paraprofessional was hired so that reference librarians will be "on call" while they tend to other responsibilities, such as collection development or creation of tutorials, the supervisor should impart this information. ("The library did a formal work assessment and discovered that librarians need to be spending time away from the desk buying books for the collection. We have hired you to staff the desk because we believe it is important to have someone at the desk to answer basic questions and to help with the computer, printers, and other technology. You will be trained on how and when to ask the librarian to help you.") An understanding of this up front will alleviate any misunderstandings or possible resentment as to why the librarians are not at the desk (DiMarco, 2005). The paraprofessional will also need to know what items are at the reference desk and work area and what purpose those items serve. Again, a checklist of items will help the paraprofessional remember items in the area and can serve as a reference until the information is mastered (Figure 4.5). When going over the items, it is important to emphasize policies when applicable.

Discussed During Orientation

1. Reference Desk Counter
   - Selected supplies (scissors, tape, three-hole punch, staplers, pencil sharpener)
   - Statistics sheet
   - Reference desk schedule
   - Library hours
   - Reference desk printer
   - Telephone
2. Reference desk drawers and cabinet
   - Photocopier keys
   - Supplies for reference printer
   - Lost and found
3. Shelf behind reference desk
   - Library of Congress Subject Headings
   - Reference Policy Manual
   - Handouts (map of libraries, instructions on logging into WiFi, library Calendar of Events)
   - Emergency procedures notebook
   - Road atlas
   - *U.S. and News and World Reports* rankings
   - *Consumer Reports Buying Guide*
4. File cabinet
   - Current Sunday classified section
   - Master copies of database tip sheets
   - Signage (out-of-order signage for computers, printers)
   - Incident reports
5. Ready reference shelves
   - New reference books
   - Handouts
   - Ready reference books
   - Shelf for patron pick up (two-day hold only)

Figure 4.5. List of Reference Desk Items

There are supplies at the reference desk; does the reference desk hand out scissors or paper clips if the patrons ask for them? There is a space on the shelf for books set aside for patrons; how long are the books kept there? Why are the Sunday classifieds kept apart from the newspaper? Are patrons permitted to use the telephone at the desk?

It is also advisable for the supervisor to review the training that the paraprofessional will receive, give the paraprofessional a schedule of the training, and provide details on how training will proceed. The supervisor should discuss the observation time at the reference desk, explaining what the paraprofessional should expect and how to observe unobtrusively, emphasizing that he or she will learn a great deal just by observing. The supervisor should offer suggestions about how to respond to patrons who ask the paraprofessional for help.

While there may be an urge to fill every minute with imparting information, the paraprofessional will need some "down time" to absorb and to get situated. A good way to provide this break is to provide time for the paraprofessional to set up his or her work space and to review and explore materials more thoroughly. It is also important that paraprofessional have some time to socialize with coworkers, as socialization is an important aspect of orientation. Employees should have opportunities to get to know their coworkers in an informal setting and to discuss their activities in an unstructured environment, such as a coffee hour or party. In a reference department, socialization is particularly important because the staff often work together as a team (Woodard, 2001). The initial period of orientation is also a time for the supervisor and to get to know the employee better. It is helpful for the supervisor to meet frequently with the paraprofessional to begin the training process, answer any questions, get to know one another, and establish a good rapport.

ORIENTATION SESSIONS

Once the initial housekeeping details are in order, the supervisor can begin the more job-specific orientation sessions. These may include a tour of the library with a worksheet to assess any gaps in coverage, discussing the philosophy of the library and of reference service, and explaining standards and expectations.

TOUR

A general tour of the library will enable the paraprofessional to begin answering directional questions at the reference desk, as well as introduce him or her to library services and collections. It is important that paraprofessionals gain familiarity with and understanding of their work environment. Therefore, the employees should receive a tour soon after beginning work. The supervisor is a good choice to provide the tour, but allowing another library employee to do so provides the paraprofessional time to get to know that employee. This could be someone in the department who is at the same level or with whom the paraprofessional will be working closely.

It is helpful to write down the tour details; the paraprofessional can add the material to the training manual for easy reference. Writing out the tour also ensures that the tour will proceed through the library in a logical fashion and that everything that needs to be pointed out is included. Other persons should review the tour plans and offer suggestions. A tour that returns to the same area several times because the tour guide suddenly recalls something important that was omitted is a tour that is confusing and a tour that does not leave a good impression. The tour should include the exterior of the building. Where is the library in relation to the surrounding area (community, campus, etc.)? Information about parking is crucial. Also, if the library building includes noteworthy architectural details, artwork, furniture, or plaques, the tour guide should point these out and provide the paraprofessional with appropriate information for future referral; patrons may notice these items and have questions. When planning the tour, it is important to strike a balance between including all information that is immediately relevant to the job and overwhelming the employee with details. The finer points can be reserved for the departmental introductions. An example of a written library tour is provided in Figure 4.6.

I. First Floor

The public entrance to the library faces east, opposite the park. The library parking lot is on the west side of the building. Limited street parking is available.

A. Lobby

1. Community Meeting Room: To the right of the lobby (south) is the community meeting room, which seats 25 persons. As the name indicates, it is for community use for things such as meetings, small classes, and book discussion groups. Reservations are handled by the director.

2. Auditorium: To the left of the lobby (north) is the auditorium, which seats 200 and is for performances and larger lectures. Reservations are also handled by the director.

3. Exhibit cases: There are two exhibit cases, which are available for community use. Persons wishing to use these should speak with the director.

4. Restrooms and public phones: The public restrooms and phones are in the lobby.

B. Circulation Desk

The first public service desk the public sees is the circulation desk.

1. This is where patrons check out and return books.

2. This is where patrons pick up patron-placed holds and interlibrary loan requests. Books that the librarians put aside for patrons are kept at the second floor reference desk.

Figure 4.6. Tour

3. This is where patrons negotiate and pay fines.

4. This is where patrons acquire new or replacement library cards.

5. Behind the desk is the safe. The person in charge of the circulation desk handles the cash.

Directly around each corner of the circulation desk are stairs to the second floor. The second floor is also accessible by the elevator, which is on the left hand side of the first floor.

C. Children and Young Adults Department

To the right (south) of the circulation desk is the Children and Young Adults Department.

1. This department has its own circulating fiction and nonfiction collection, as well as its own reference collection.

2. This department has its own reference desk.

3. Special collections include the Newbery and Caldecott collections and the collection of holiday-themed books.

4. The DVD collection for children is kept in the Audio Visual Department.

5. Anyone can check out books from this collection.

Point out location of computer workstations, noting what software applications are loaded on each computer.

D. Audio Visual Department

To the left (north) of the circulation desk is the A/V Department. All DVDs and CDs are kept here. The library no longer collects VHS format or cassette tapes.

1. Children's DVD collection: This contains both educational and entertainment DVDs. The educational DVDs are arranged in call number order; the entertainment DVDs are arranged by title.

2. Foreign film collection: All arranged by title.

3. Music CD collection: In call number order.

4. All other DVDs: Also educational and entertainment DVDs, arranged in call number order or in title order.

Note position of elevator relative to A/V Department and take elevator to second floor.

II. Second Floor

The elevator door opens up to the left (west) of the Adult Services reference desk. The book shelves directly in front of the elevator contain the following:

- phone directories,
- the test book collection, and
- and the auto manual reference collection.

A. Adult Reference Desk

The front of the adult reference desk looks directly out onto the double staircases. Patrons coming up the stairs have a choice of two desks to approach, periodicals to the left (south), adult reference to the (right) north. Be aware that patrons may mistake the periodicals desk for reference and might be sent to the adult reference desk from periodicals.

Figure 4.6. Tour (*Continued*)

B. Local History Collection

Behind the desk is a local history collection that is building use only. There two tables for people to work at. Photocopying of materials is allowed. Collection is in call number order.

C. Nonfiction Collection

The nonfiction book collection is on the north half of the floor. Reference can be found on the shelves directly behind the reference desk. Circulating collection is across the aisle. Both collections are shelved in call number order.

D. Current and Bound Periodicals (Magazines)

These are shelved directly behind the periodicals desk and are in alphabetical order by title.

E. Fiction Collection

The fiction collection is on the south half of the floor. This collection is arranged alphabetically by author.

Note locations of computer workstations on floor and point out what software packages are loaded on these computers.

Walk back to the elevator and take it down to the basement.

III. Basement

The basement is not a public service floor, but it has many functions that impact public service.

A. Book Processing

New books are processed here. It is important to check this table on a weekly basis to see what is being added to the collection.

B. Book Sorting and Reshelving

Books turned in at the circulation desk are sorted to be reshelved here. If you and/or the patron can't find a book on the shelf, check here for the book. Always let the patron know this is what you are doing! The books are in order on the shelves and carts as they are upstairs: nonfiction books are in call number order, fiction books are in order by the author's last name.

C. Staff Lounge

This area is for staff use while on break.

Figure 4.6. Tour (*Continued*)

Once the paraprofessional has had a tour of the library, it is useful to test his or her knowledge before permitting him or her to answer directional questions at the reference desk. This can also be a time to evaluate how well the employee understands some basic reference policies and procedures. A worksheet that includes items that the supervisor thinks are important can be an excellent tool in determining such basic understanding. Figure 4.7 is an example of such a worksheet based on the tour described in Figure 4.6.

Answer the following questions to the best of your ability. When the worksheet is completed, return it to me. Remember: this is not a quiz or a test, and will not be used in evaluations; this is simply a training device.

Short Answer

1. Name three things patrons can do at the circulation desk.

2. What is the difference between the auditorium and the community meeting room?

3. How are the fiction books arranged?

4. How long do patrons have to pick up holds they have placed?

Multiple Choice

5. Which of the following can be found on the second floor?
   a. current periodicals
   b. back issues of periodicals
   c. microform readers and printers
   d. local history collection
   e. all of the above

True or False

6. Patrons negotiate fines at the second floor reference desk.

7. Entertainment videos are arranged by call number.

8. The exhibit cases are for library staff use only.

9. Adults can check out books in the children's collection.

10. The local history collection is building use only.

Figure 4.7. Library Tour Worksheet

Demonstrate how you would locate the information on the library Web site:

1. What are the library's hours?

2. What are the steps for patrons to access their online account?

3. What are the loan periods for various library materials?

4. What are the fines?

5. How can a patron get a library card?

6. What is the bookmobile schedule?

7. What are the children's programs offered?

8. Are there driving directions to the library?

Figure 4.8. Library Web Site Worksheet

LIBRARY WEB SITE

Most libraries now have Web sites, where patrons and staff alike can learn about and access library services. There will a specific training module about accessing library services available through the Web site, but initially, the supervisor should give the paraprofessional an overview of the basic information that can be found on the library's Web site and then provide time to explore it. Not only will this exercise reinforce the information being presented in orientation and training, but the paraprofessional may have to walk patrons through finding this information, either over the telephone or in person. As with the library tour, testing the paraprofessional's knowledge of the Web site can be useful. Figure 4.8 provides a test on the paraprofessional's knowledge of the Web site.

DEPARTMENT INTRODUCTIONS

Department introductions are more in depth than library tours because they allow the staff of other library departments, sections, or branches to introduce the paraprofessional to the personnel, policies, procedures, and resources of that area. The supervisor needs to determine the best time during the orientation to schedule these visits. If the reference department often refers patrons to other departments, visits should occur in the beginning of the program. Also, if the training needs include becoming familiar with the policies of a particular department (circulation, interlibrary loan), the paraprofessional needs an early introduction to the staff and tasks of those departments. However, if there is little interaction between the reference department and another department, visits can take place after the paraprofessional is comfortable with his or her primary job tasks. Spacing the visits out might enable the paraprofessional to better digest the information presented (Davis, 1994).

Department introductions should familiarize the paraprofessional with the personnel, activities, procedures, and policies of other library sections. The reference desk is often the first point of contact for patrons who need services from or information about other department; information provided in these visits should enable the paraprofessional to answer patron questions more effectively and make better referrals. The paraprofessional will also have a better idea of the work relationship between the reference department and other departments and how the library functions as a whole.

Prior to formally scheduling the visits, the supervisor should determine what the paraprofessional should learn in each departmental introduction. It is important to keep in mind that the paraprofessional probably does not have the benefit of an MLS or may never have worked in a library. Following are some questions to consider:

When is this department staffed? This is especially important if the department is not staffed during the same hours as the reference department. In this case, the paraprofessional should learn what times that department is closed when reference is open and be informed about how this might impact reference service. If the public does not have access to the materials or services, the paraprofessional should be aware of options for the patron, such as contacting the department by e-mail or filling out a call-back slip.

What is done in this department and who works there? The paraprofessional needs to understand what tasks other library departments are responsible for. This information is useful for responding to patron questions and/or making correct referrals. For example, after learning who manages reserves, the paraprofessional will know to whom questions about reserves should be referred. The paraprofessional should know the names of the employees in other departments and whether or not these employees have particular responsibilities. For example, the interlibrary loan department borrows books from other libraries and lends to other libraries. However, within that department, there may be one person who is responsible for lending books from the library and another who is responsible for borrowing books on behalf of library patrons. If patrons approach the reference desk in search of particular library employees, either by name or by function, the paraprofessional can correctly direct the patron to the correct location or department.

What is the work flow in this department? The paraprofessional should understand how work moves through the library. What happens to a book once it gets returned to the library? Where does the book go before it gets back on the shelf? Are options available for the patron to get a book that has been returned but not yet shelved? If the employee is familiar with the work flow of other library departments, he or she will know what steps to take when answering patron questions that concern those department's activities.

Are there resources in the department that reference department personnel should know about? Some reference sources may not be housed in the reference section. For example, *Ulrich's Periodicals Directory* may be kept at the periodicals desk, or *Something About the Author* may be in the children's section. If the reference department refers patrons to sources that are not in the reference collection, the paraprofessional must learn where these resources are housed and why they are not kept at references. The supervisor should explain the coverage and use of these sources so that he or she can confidently refer patrons to the sources when necessary. If the paraprofessional is touring a library division or department with its own materials, the paraprofessional should be made aware if there are restrictions on the use of those materials. For example, some materials may not circulate, may not be taken to another area of the library, may not be photocopies, or may require some form of identification for use.

Which patrons and questions should be referred to this department? If there are questions that the reference department consistently refers to another library department, the paraprofessional should be made aware of those questions and the reasons other departments handle the questions. Are all the guides to using the federal census kept with the census microfilm in the microfilm department? Must all fines be negotiated and paid at the circulation desk? Also, if the department wishes reference staff to call before sending patrons to its area, this should be communicated to the paraprofessional during the visit to the department.

What should not be referred to this department? There may be patrons who should not be referred to a specific department. For example, some library services may not be available to all library patrons (e.g., available only to faculty, students, and staff of a college or university). Special issues of periodicals such as rankings by *U.S. News and World Report* or parts of the newspaper, such as the Sunday classified ads, might be kept at the reference desk, not at the periodicals desk. The employee must know the exceptions.

Does this department call before referring patrons to reference? If reference is called, the paraprofessional should be told how these phone calls are to be handled. How much information about the patron's information need will the caller provide? Is a reference staff member expected to find an answer while the patron is traveling to reference? Will the paraprofessional have to repeat the reference interview? Will the patron have some sort of printout or referral slip? Where or to whom will the patron be referred, to the reference desk or to the staff member who took the call?

Once it is known what must be covered in the department visits, the supervisor must arrange the visits. Ideally, the supervisor would have contacted the departments prior to the employee's start date to give advance notice that tours would be necessary. At this point, provide more information about the purpose of the training; communicate what the desired topics to be covered are and ask if the department head has suggestions for additional information that should be included. The presenter may need to prepare handouts to supplement what he or she will be discussing. The supervisor should schedule the department visit during a time that is convenient for the reference desk, the paraprofessional, and the department to be visited. Inform the paraprofessional when and where the session will take place, whom the paraprofessional will meet, and what the topic will be.

Some of what is presented in the department visit may repeat information the staff member has already received; the repetition will reinforce the information for the paraprofessional. The visits should clarify other department's policies and/or procedures; information could prove useful in explaining some situations to patrons. For instance, it might not be obvious why it takes a week to get a new best seller to the public shelves once the book is received, but a visit to the technical services area would explain why this occurs.

Preferably, the supervisor or designated trainer should accompany the paraprofessional to the department visits. This provides an opportunity to point out connections to the reference department as well as prepare for any follow-up questions that might occur. This will also provide a chance to prompt the presenter if something that the paraprofessional needs to know has been omitted.

After the department introduction, the supervisor should ask the paraprofessional for comments on the visits and the presentations and for questions about the material covered. The supervisor should also reflect on the session; did the presenter include everything that needed to be covered? If questions about the department persist, a follow up visit should be scheduled.

Helpful Sources

Encourage new paraprofessionals to be aware of resources that apply to or guide library service, such as:

- Library Bill of Rights (available from the American Library Association's Web site: www.ala.org)
- American Library Association's Code of Ethics (available from the American Library Association's Web site: www.ala.org)
- Behavioral Guidelines for Reference and Information Service Providers (see Appendix)

PHILOSOPHY OF SERVICE

It is important to acquaint the paraprofessional with the library's philosophy of public service early in the orientation process. In order to become successful at reference work, paraprofessionals need to learn how to deal with the public effectively. A memo provided to the employee in the beginning can highlight what is important and start the paraprofessional thinking about the library's philosophy of service. For example, the library's general philosophy of service may be a statement, such as, "The reference staff strives to provide accurate information and materials in response to requests from library patrons in an efficient, courteous, and timely manner." But this may be carried out differently, depending on what is going on at the library. If the library is very busy, the service will differ than if the library is experiencing a slower time. However, different service does not mean that one service is good and one is bad. The paraprofessional will need to understand how to handle situations so that any problems or misunderstandings can be addressed. For example, a library's philosophy of service may be not to do the research for the patrons but to instruct patrons in the use of sources so that patrons can become more self-sufficient in using the library. The philosophy may be that reference staff provides service to patrons in the order that requests are received; persons in the library do not take precedence over those on the telephone. This information needs to be communicated to the paraprofessional.

The philosophy of service discussion can begin with case studies related to public service, a role-playing session followed by a discussion, or by simply asking the new employee for a definition of public service. Several sample situations for use in starting case studies or role-plays follow. These can be adapted to a specific library. The "correct" answers to these situations will depend on the philosophy, policies, and procedures for individual libraries.

> **Case 1:** A woman is angry because the tax forms she needs are not available in the distribution rack. In these cases, patrons have the option to make photocopies from a master copy. This makes the woman angrier. She demands that you make the photocopies for her, stating that she shouldn't have to pay for forms just so that she can pay the government, because she's already giving money to the government. How do you respond?

> **Case 2:** A patron telephones, begins to describe a number of physical symptoms, and asks whether it is possible that she has a certain illness. What are the next steps to take?

> **Case 3:** A man who is accompanied by his school-aged daughter approaches the desk with two books from the local history collection, which is deemed "building use only" and does not circulate. The circulation department will not let him check the books out and has sent him back to the reference desk. You explain to him that the books do not circulate. He becomes angrier, saying that his daughter needs the books for her history fair assignment and his tax dollars pay for these books that the library is not letting her use. How do you respond?

> **Case 4:** A patron with a heavy accent asks you a reference question. You have asked her to repeat the question several times but still cannot understand what she needs. How can you proceed?

> **Case 5:** The library has recently switched its print subscription to a personal investing resource to an online version. Mr. Green, an older, longtime library patron who has used the print resource weekly, is very upset. He complains that he is not comfortable using a computer and that this information is very important to him. He demands that the library reinstate the print subscription so that he can get what he needs. How do you respond?

Case 6: A mother comes to the reference desk to complain about a patron using the Adult Internet stations. She claims she and her small children saw a man viewing what she considers to be pornography. She claims the she is now uncomfortable bringing her children to the library, that it is no longer "family friendly." An elderly lady chimes in to agree. What do you do?

Case 7: It is a busy Saturday, and there is a line of patrons waiting for reference service. The telephone rings, and a patron on the other end states that she is disabled and cannot come to the library and requires assistance that will take a good amount of time. How do you handle this situation?

Figure 4.9 is a sample "philosophy of service" memo that can be tailored and used in a discussion about service philosophy. In addition to the memo's points about approachability, interest, listening, and follow-up, the supervisor may want to include the following:

- The patron is the first priority. Try to make responses patron oriented. Library policies exist to meet the needs of the majority of the patrons.
- All patrons should be treated the same in accordance with library policies.
- Try to put the patron at ease throughout the entire reference transaction.
- Keep the patron informed about what you are doing to answer his or her question, and do not make patrons wait for extended periods of time.
- If you cannot answer the question, admit this to the patron and suggest what other action can be taken. Referrals count as a correct answer.
- Patrons with concerns or complaints should be taken to private areas and perhaps be referred to a supervisor or department manager.

Encourage the paraprofessional to discuss any situation she or he would like feedback on or clarification about and emphasize that this will be an ongoing learning process; even seasoned employees still learn about providing service.

It is constructive to brief the paraprofessional about the library's typical patrons. Identify common social, economic, or educational backgrounds. If there is a group of patrons resistant to the online catalog or other electronic resources, they should be identified for the paraprofessional and strategies for working with them should be discussed. Remind

TO: Reference Assistants

SUBJECT: Ten Tips for Service Success

We are glad to have you join the reference staff, where public service is our first priority. You are now a member of our team and will help in our efforts to provide our patrons with courteous, efficient, and effective service. Following are some of the most important guidelines to keep in mind to help you provide the best possible service to our patrons. These are not all our guidelines, just a cheat sheet to get you started. More detailed information can be found in the "Reference Department Policies and Procedures Manual;" you can also consult Appendix One of the manual "Behavioral Guidelines for Reference and Information Service Providers." As always, please let me know if I can be of any assistance.

1. Be approachable. When you are scheduled at the reference desk, public service comes before other duties. Please be friendly and welcoming.
2. Listen carefully to what the patron is asking and demonstrate interest.
3. Accompany patrons to the computer and/or the reference stacks and instruct them on the use of resources.
4. There are no limits to the amount of time you spend with a patron. However, please keep in mind the traffic at the desk. If there are a lot of patrons, you will need to judge how much time you can spend with each patron. It may be necessary to get a patron started and then return later to check up.
5. Requests for help are taken in the order received. Be sure to acknowledge patrons waiting for help. If you wish to see whether the people who are waiting have a quick question, always ask the patron you are helping if he or she minds you providing quick, verbal assistance to other customers.
6. Always follow up with patrons, asking them if they found what they need.
7. Reference transactions are confidential.
8. Teamwork is an essential part of reference. Do not hesitate to ask for help if you do not know the answer. If you feel something is taking too long or if you feel overwhelmed, be sure to request assistance from one of the librarians. It is better to hand the question over to someone else rather than give an incorrect or incomplete answer. **REFERRALS COUNT AS A CORRECT ANSWER.**
9. If it is quiet at the desk, please rove through the computer area to see if there are patrons who need help.
10. Always cite your sources.

Figure 4.9. Philosophy of Service Memo

the paraprofessional about the "flow" of the reference department (discussed during orientation to the desk) and point out how the clientele may change with time of day or time of year.

Another important aspect of public service is learning how to handle difficult patrons. Paraprofessionals should be trained in this so that they will feel equipped to handle these situations and so that they feel the library supports them. Good orientation techniques for dealing with problem patrons include role-playing and discussion, and case studies. A written reminder, such as the one in Figure 4.10, can also be helpful for the paraprofessional.

TO: Reference Assistants

SUBJECT: Dealing with Difficult Patrons

One of the realities of working public service is difficult patrons. No matter how long you have worked in public service, it is never easy to encounter an unhappy or angry patron. Below are some strategies to help you deal with difficult patrons. Please feel free to contact me with any questions or concerns you may have.

1. Even though the patron is taking out his or her frustration on you, try not to take it personally.
2. Try to remain friendly at all times. Do not become confrontational.
3. Do not try to resolve the complaint in front of other patrons. Instead, take the patron to a private area.
4. Show sympathy for the patron's situation without criticizing library policy; Remember that you are representing the library.
5. Listen carefully and attentively to the whole complaint. By listening you demonstrate to the patron that you have respect for him or her and the complaint.
6. Never argue with a patron. Instead, disagree diplomatically, e.g.,"I never thought of it that way."
7. Apologize. You don't have to apologize for the policy; you can, however, tell the patron "I'm sorry you feel that way."
8. Be flexible and try to find other avenues to meet the patron's need.
9. If you cannot resolve the complaint, tell the patron you think he or she will be better served by getting the person in charge.
10. Remember to never touch a patron.
11. If you feel you are in any physical danger, call the police. (Rubin, 2000)

Figure 4.10. Difficult Patrons Memo

PERFORMANCE STANDARDS AND EXPECTATIONS

Each library, and each supervisor, has standards of work performance and expectations of the library staff. It is the supervisor's responsibility to let employees know that behavior and work performance are important; these play a major role in the performance evaluation. Paraprofessionals will be more productive and will feel more secure in their jobs if they know what the supervisor expects of them. Therefore, the supervisor should be honest and forthright in identifying performance standards with them. Many performance expectations for the paraprofessionals, along with the competency descriptions, might have been formulated during the planning stages of training (Chapter 2).

The supervisor should schedule a meeting with the new staff member to discuss performance expectations (both short-term and long-term), ensure that they are understood, and clear up any possible concerns or misunderstandings. The paraprofessional should receive written copies of the expectations and/or the competency description for future reference. The supervisor should remind the paraprofessional that he or she will receive training with the idea of meeting those performance expectations.

It is helpful to explain the performance evaluation procedures to new employees during the orientation process. Give them a copy of the performance evaluation form and make it clear how performance is rated in each category. For example, in the area of punctuality, arriving five minutes early is satisfactory, but arriving more than five minutes late more than once each month is unacceptable. In addition to discussing the performance evaluation, the probationary period and any accompanying evaluation should be covered (DiMarco, 2005).

Proper orientation and further training can only benefit the library and the patrons being served. It is essential to spend time creating a successful orientation program to get new employees off to a good start. The beginning days and weeks of a paraprofessional's employment are vital to his or her learning the proper skills, being effective at his or her job, and having a good attitude about the library and his or her work. A well-developed orientation program will ensure that they become fully functioning members of the reference department as quickly as possible.

> "Above all . . . make sure new employees get this message: 'We are glad you made the decision to work for us, and we are glad you are here'." (Gustafson, 2005, p. 41)

REFERENCES

"Checklist for New Employee Orientation." 2000. *Library Personnel News* 13, no. 1–2 (Spring/Summer):15–16. Provides a sample of checklist of items that employers should introduce to new employees.

Davis, H. Scott. 1994. *New Employee Orientation: A How-To-Do-It Manual for Librarians*. New York: Neal-Schuman Publishers. An entire book devoted to planning, running, and evaluating employee orientations.

DiMarco, Scott R. 2005. "Practicing the Golden Rule: Creating a Win-Win New Employee Orientation." *College and Research Libraries News* 66, no. 2 (Fall):110–113. DiMarco gives a concise but thorough overview of planning for orientation.

Gustafson, Kristin. 2005. "A Better Welcome Mat." *Training* 42, no. 6 (June): 41.

Rubin, Rhea Joyce. 2000. "Defusing the Angry Patron." *Library Mosaics* 11, no. 3 (May/June):14–15. In an article aimed at support staff, Rhea Joyce Rubin offers practical tips on how to handle angry patrons. In addition, she also delves into the emotion of anger and what it is all about.

Rubin, Richard E. 1991. *Human Resource Management in Libraries: Theory and Practice*. New York: Neal-Schuman. Rubin puts orientation into the larger context of hiring employees.

Weingart, Sandra J., Carol A. Kochan, and Anne Hedrich. 1998. "Safeguarding Your Investment: Effective Orientation for New Employees." *Library Administration & Management* 12, no. 3 (Summer): 156–158. This article is another source of what to cover during orientation.

Woodard, Beth S. 2001. "Reference Service Improvement: Staff Orientation, Training, and Continuing Education." In *Reference and Information Services*. 3rd ed., edited by Richard E. Bopp and Linda C. Smith, 210–244. Englewood, CO: Libraries Unlimited. Woodard's overview of planning for training includes information about orientation and its place within the bigger part of training.

Young, Heartsill (ed.). 1983. *The ALA Glossary of Library and Information Science*. Chicago, IL: American Library Association.

5 BASIC SKILLS

> The paraprofessional will need to learn many tasks, not all of which can be taught at once. Basic skills can be those tasks that will be done frequently, such as searching the online catalog, and/or those that are truly basic, such as call number training.

This chapter presents modules and checklists for basic skills: tasks the paraprofessional should master soon after beginning employment. These sections are:

1. Online Catalog Training
2. Web Services (self-service points available through a library's home page)
3. Evaluating Internet Sources
4. Call Number Training (Library of Congress and Dewey Decimal)

---

1. ONLINE CATALOG TRAINING

OBJECTIVES

1. Be able to define the catalog.
2. Given the exact title of the book or author name or call number and using the catalog, correctly determine 95 percent of the time whether or not the library owns the book.
3. From a holdings record, determine where the book is located and whether it is on the shelf.
4. From a record, determine whether the library owns a particular periodical, in what format (print or electronic) and for what years.

Online public access catalogs differ widely among libraries, due to individual libraries' customization and implementation. This individualization makes it difficult to tailor a training module for online catalog training. The checklist below is intended to help you consider some of the topics that might be covered in a discussion about using an online catalog.

CHECKLIST

1. Define the catalog (Online catalogs help patrons determine what materials the library owns and locate those materials.)
2. Explain what types of materials can be found in the catalog.
   a. Books
      • nonfiction
      • fiction
   b. Periodicals (not the names of specific articles)
      • print
      • electronic
   c. Sound recordings
   d. Video recordings
   e. Government documents
   f. Music scores
3. Demonstrate the ways in which the catalog can be searched using a single search term.
   a. Author

    b. Title

    c. Subject

    d. Call number

    e. Journal title

    f. Keyword

    g. How to turn a keyword search into a subject search

    h. How to find short stories and plays (title or keyword search)

    i. Other access points

4. For each type of search in section 3, explain the following.

    a. What pieces of information are found in the list of results?

    b. What additional information is found in the individual record display?

    c. What elements are hyperlinked?

    d. What happens when one clicks on a link?

    e. What is the sort order for the results list?

    f. Can the results list be resorted in a different order (i.e., alphabetical, chronological?)

5. Demonstrate how the catalog can be searched using different search terms and Boolean operators

6. For special types of formats, show how a search can be limited to find only:

    a. Music score

    b. DVD

    c. Music CD

    d. Audio book CD

    e. Electronic resource

7. From the holdings information in the full record, locate:

    a. Call numbers

    b. Location of book

    c. Circulation status

8. For a periodical, instruct how to

    a. Find out whether the library owns the periodical in print, in electronic format, and/or both formats.

    b. For a print periodical, determine what years are available and where those issues are located.

    c. Access the electronic copy.

2. WEB SERVICES

OBJECTIVES

1. Know how to find all self-service points on the Web site.
2. Using the Web site, be able to show how to perform each self-service task.

Libraries make many of their services available through their Web sites. The paraprofessional should be familiar with all of these services so that she or he can provide assistance and demonstrate to patrons. The supervisor will need to comb over the Web site and identify all self-service points for patrons (excluding searching the libraries' catalogs and databases, which will be covered elsewhere) and make a checklist of what the paraprofessional should understand. Below is a sample checklist.

CHECKLIST

1. How to locate class reserves
   a. By instructor's name only
   b. By course name only
2. How to view a patron account
   a. How to renew books
3. How to log into a database remotely
   a. How to report a problem logging in
4. How to use the library's virtual reference service and what the patron can expect
   a. E-mail
   b. Chat and/or IM
5. How to fill out an interlibrary loan request
   a. Book
   b. Journal article
6. How to view an e-book
7. How to locate e-journals

8. How to request a book the library owns that is currently not on the shelf
    a. Hold
    b. Recall
    c. Request from storage
9. How to locate various request forms
10. How to book a meeting room
11. How to schedule a consultation
12. How to request an instruction session
13. How to suggest a purchase

3. EVALUATING INTERNET SOURCES

OBJECTIVES

1. From memory, identify at least four criteria for Web site evaluation.
2. Any time the decision is made to use an Internet resource to answer a reference question, always use the criteria to evaluate the Web sites.

Library staff can expect to use and recommend Web sites when providing reference service. The paraprofessional must learn how to evaluate Web information. The checklist below serves as a guide to evaluating Web sites and provides clues of what to look for in a Web site. Emphasize to the paraprofessional that before using or providing information found on a Web page, the following criteria should be considered to evaluate the credibility of the Web site. The staff member should NOT use his or own personal standards when evaluating a Web site.

AUTHORITY

Questions to ask:

- Who is the author or creator of the page?
- What are his or her credentials and can they be verified?
- Could the credentials be fabricated?
- What organization is sponsoring the Web page?

Encourage the paraprofessional to always verify who sponsors the site. The domain name can provide good information.

- Sites ending in ".gov" are sponsored by the government.
- Sites ending in ".org" are sponsored by nonprofit organizations.
- Sites ending in ".edu" are institutions of higher learning.
- Sites ending in ".com" are commercial sites.
- Sites that have a tilde (~) are usually an indication that the Web site is someone's personal home page. This does not mean the page should not be used. It could be the home page of a professor or other expert.

Another approach to verify site sponsorship is to look for an "about this site" link or something similar. Determine whether the Web site provides the author's qualifications, biography, or affiliations.

ACCURACY

Questions to ask:

- Does the author support the information he or she uses?
- Can the information be verified by a print resource or its electronic equivalent?
- Does the author cite his or her sources?

The paraprofessional should look for links and/or citations to sources consulted. Are these sources well-known and authoritative? Do other pages on similar topics also cite these sources? The staff member should be wary of a Web page where it is difficult to check the sources.

CURRENCY

Questions to ask:

- Is the date of creation or revision clear?
- Is the information up-to-date?

The staff member should look for a date on the Web page that indicates when the page was created or last modified. A site with many broken links is a site that could be out of date. The paraprofessional should also be aware of the discipline. Information in science, technology, and business fields ages quickly; information in the humanities and social sciences age less quickly. In some cases, older information can be perfectly valid.

PURPOSE

Questions to ask:

- What is the purpose of the page?
- Who is the intended audience?

The paraprofessional should try to determine what the author's intent is. It could be to advertise, to entertain, to inform, to persuade, etc. Some Web pages have multiple intents, many sites provide free information that is authoritative but also encourage site visitors to buy a product. Some satire sites closely resemble authoritative news sources.

OBJECTIVITY

Question to ask:

- Is the author being objective or biased?

The paraprofessional should look at what information is provided and what might be omitted, as well as the tone of the Web site. Is the information presented in a moderate and balanced manner? Or is the tone extreme? If the purpose of the Web site is to advocate or to persuade, then biased information is not necessarily a negative point. But the paraprofessional must take that viewpoint into account and consider providing the patron with an equal, opposing opinion. Objectivity is closely tied to the purpose of the Web site.

EXERCISE

Using the criteria above, evaluate the following Web sites:

www.peta.org
www.theonion.com
www.heritage.org

4. CALL NUMBER TRAINING

OBJECTIVES

1. Define purpose(s) of call numbers.
2. From memory, be able to put call numbers in order with no errors.

A call number of a book tells exactly where a book is located on the shelf. It also groups together books with a similar subject on the shelf. Each book has a unique call number, like an address for a house. It is important to understand how call numbers are constructed and how they are put into order so that you can assist patrons in locating books on the shelf.

LIBRARY OF CONGRESS CALL NUMBERS

Anatomy of a Library of Congress Call Number

Library of Congress Call numbers are a combination of letters and numbers. Each call number may contain three, four, or five lines.

1. The first line of the call number defines the general subject and subclass. This might be one, two, or three letters.
2. The second line defines a narrower subtopic within the specified class. This second line may be followed by a related line that is a decimal number; these decimal numbers are used to further organize large subject areas.
3. The third line, known as the cutter number, represents the author's name, geographic area, or the title of the work. This is a combination of a letter and number.
4. The fourth line shows publication year (may not appear on older books).
5. The fifth line gives the copy number (if the library has multiple copies of the same book, these will be identified by a copy number) or volume number.

How Are They Arranged?

1. **Alphabetically,** based on the letter in the top line.

   A comes before AE
   AE comes before B
   BS comes before BX
   R comes before TX

2. Works with the same first line are then arranged **numerically** based on the second line. If the second line is followed by a decimal number, arrange it in decimal order:

(QA comes before	QA
76.76	76.8)

3. For the third line, read the letter alphabetically and the number as a decimal. The following call numbers are in order.

HV	HV	HV	HV	HV	HV	HV	HV	HV	HV
6080	6080	6080	6080	6080	6080	6080	6080	6080	6080
.N5	.O45	.O46	.P32	.P33	.P66	.P825	.P827	.P828	.P83

4. If the year appears, the order is chronological.

Practice: Put the following call numbers in order.

Basic

a. AG 6 .N49 2002

b. D11.5 .C48 2005

c. F192.3.W33 2006

d. Q180.N334 1995

e. BF76.7.P83 2001

f. AS911.A2 F653 2007

g. L901.032 2006

h. E154.5.N37 2005

i. AY67.N5 W7 2007

j. HC110.P63 G69 1999

k. JA51.I57 2007

l. PN6081.D27 2002b

Advanced

a. NA737.W7 H89 2004

b. NA737.W7 S3

c. NA737.W7 W7 1994

d. NA737.W7 L55 1996

e. NA737.W7 S433 1997

f. NA737.W7 S32 1992x

g. NA737.W7 L57 1986

h. NA737.W7 W76

i. NA737.W7 H64 1992

j. NA737.W7 S43 1992

Answers

Basic: a, f, i, e, b, h, c, j, k, g, l, d

Advanced: i, a, d, g, b, f, j, e, c, h

DEWEY DECIMAL NUMBERS

Anatomy of a Dewey Decimal Call Number

Dewey Decimal call numbers are mostly numbers, and can be comprised of up to three parts.

1. The first part, always a number, is based on the subject of the book. This is comprised of three numbers, followed by a decimal number.
2. The second line, the cutter number, always begins with a letter, which usually refers to the author's last name.

How Are Dewey Decimal Numbers Arranged?

File one decimal at a time; in the Dewey Decimal system, books are filed by digit, not by whole number. A good analogy is money: $150.50 is more than $150.05. Adding zeros to the numbers may help clarify things.

331.78**00**
331.06**50**
331.30**90**
331.0166
331.2**000**

File the second line alphabetically.

Exercises

Put the following Dewey Decimal numbers in order

a. 371.5 Zer	f. 303.483 Sei
b. 133.1 Pri	g. 002.075 Lan
c. 005.72 Bin	h. 364.1523 Kon
d. 364.1523 Kin	i. 133.10975 Duf
e. 371.46 Mil	j. 005.713769 Pf

a. 641.5638 Car	f. 641.568 Bon
b. 641.522 Dew	g. 641.5635 Coo
c. 641.5092 Ruh	h. 641.53 Cou
d. 641.512 Slo	i. 641.5784 For
e. 641.56311 New	j. 641.589 Gil

Answers:

g, j, c, b, i, f, d, h, e, a

c, d, b, h, e, g, a, f, i, j

RESOURCES

EVALUATING INTERNET RESOURCES

Numerous Web sites show how to evaluate resources. Some examples:

Bill and Melinda Gates Foundation. "Web Site Evaluation Resources." 2002. Available: www.webjunction.org/do/DisplayContent?id=1301. Accessed: November 2, 2007.

Duke University. "Evaluating Web Resources." Available: http://library. duke.edu/services/instruction/libraryguide/evalwebpages.html. Accessed: November 2, 2007.

Healey Library Information Literacy Tutorial. "Module 4: How to Evaluate Information on the Web." Available: /www.lib.umb.edu/ newtutorial/module4_5.html. Accessed: November 2, 2007.

Johns Hopkins University. The Sheridan Libraries. "Evaluating Information Found on the Internet." Available: www.library.jhu.edu/ researchhelp/general/evaluating/. Accessed: November 2, 2007.

CALL NUMBER TRAINING

The World Wide Web has numerous library guides and tutorials explaining each classification system, which can be found using a search engine.

Library of Congress Classification Outline. Available: www.loc.gov/ catdir/cpso/lcco/. Accessed: November 4, 2007.

Dewey Decimal Classification System. Available: www.oclc.org/dewey/ about/default.htm. Accessed: November 4, 2007.

ADVANCED SKILLS

> When designing training for advanced skills, it is important that the basics be mastered first. It is also crucial that complex tasks be broken down and described.

This chapter presents examples of modules and checklists for more advanced skills: tasks the paraprofessional could learn after mastering some of the basics (presented in Chapter 5). The sections are:

1. Article Database Training (including more advanced search skills such as Boolean searching
2. Federated Searching
3. Link Resolvers
4. Superintendent of Documents (SuDoc) Numbers

1. ARTICLE DATABASE TRAINING

OBJECTIVES

1. Be able to define what kind of information can be found in the database.
2. Name at least three ways the database can be searched.
3. Be able to identify all elements for a citation.
4. Be able to print, e-mail, or save the article and/or the citation information.

A database is simply a collection of information that is organized in an electronic format that can be searched electronically. Anyone who has ever searched iTunes, Amazon.com, or eBay has searched a database.

Databases are comprised of records. A record is a description of an individual resource database (a record for each journal article). Each of these records is comprised of fields: title, author, subjects, etc., that provides more information about the item.

Below are basic fields for databases that correspond to a unique piece of information in a journal article that can be used in searching. There may be other fields or pieces of information in a record, but these are the fundamental ones to know.

Title: the title of the article in the journal

Author (s): the authors of the article

Source: the name of the journal, magazine or newspaper that the article appears in

Subject (sometimes known as **descriptor**): a specific set of vocabulary used to describe the content of the article

Abstract: a summary of the article

Example:

Title: Amazing, Magic Searches!
Authors: Kornegay, Becky
Buchanan, Heidi
Morgan, Hiddy
Source: *Library Journal*
Subject Terms: Online catalogs
Online searching

Abstract: This article examines the use of Library of Congress subject subdivisions in keyword searches. Subdivisions can identify the format of a book's content, or define and specify relationships between topics. The article presents a list of subdivisions that could assist a librarian when searching for books about a specific topic.

Once one understands the basic fields of a database, it is possible to construct different types of searches to retrieve information.

Searching by Specific Fields

Specific fields can be a search term. For example, it is possible to do a search by article title, if a patron asks, "I was assigned this article to read. Can you help me find a copy?" or author "I need a list of articles written by Thomas Friedman." If the specific subject heading or journal name is known, it also possible to search by the corresponding fields. Simply select the appropriate field in the database, type in the information, and perform the search.

Keyword Searching

Databases usually offer the option to do a keyword search, which is a more powerful search method. A keyword usually does not correspond to a particular field or piece of information but comprises several fields. A keyword search looks for words anywhere in the record. Whereas searching by author only searches the author field, searching by title only searched the title field, a keyword search may search the author field, the title field, the subject fields, and the abstract field. Keyword searches are a good substitute for a subject search when the subject heading is unknown. Keyword may also be used as a substitute for a title or author search when there is insufficient information about the title or author.

Phrase Searching

If you want two words to appear together, e.g., "fashion design," you will need to search these as a phrase.

Boolean Operators

If a search is more complex, a simple search box will not be very effective. The best approach is to construct a search strategy using Boolean operators. Utilizing a Boolean operator is the process of linking concepts to formulate an effective search strategy. There are three Boolean operators: AND, OR, and NOT.

"AND" links two or more terms and is useful to narrow a search. It finds all of the concepts.

Example: Searching for "child" AND "psychology" will retrieve only those records where both of these terms are present.

"OR" is helpful when expanding a search. Using OR retrieves all records containing one of the concepts, whether or not the other concepts are in the record. This tactic can be useful when using synonyms or related concepts.

Example: Clothing OR apparel OR fashion

"NOT" is used to exclude a search term.

Example: Photography NOT digital will exclude any materials on digital photography.

Now that you understand the some basics searching, you are ready to learn how to search the online catalog and databases.

CHECKLIST

1. Discuss what can be found in the particular database.
   - Subjects (specific subject, multipurpose)
   - Type of material (articles, primary sources, biographical material, etc.)
   - Full text versus citation and abstract only
2. Review some of the different database fields that can be used for searching.
   - Author
   - Title
   - Source
   - Keyword
   - Subject
   - Abstract

3. Review some of the ways a search can be limited.
   - Full text only
   - Scholarly or peer reviewed
   - Date range
   - Publication type

4. Have the paraprofessional do a search using the basic search feature.
   - Is it possible to limit this basic search to a particular field or is searching comprised only of typing something in the box?
   - Is it possible to refine the search on the results screen?
   - Is it possible to filter results by type of publication (scholarly journal, magazine, newspaper, etc.)?

5. Explain the elements of a citation from a result.
   - Author
   - Title
   - Source
   - Date of publication
   - Volume number, issue number, etc.

6. On the record, point out how to e-mail, print, save, and export a citation and/or article. Is it possible to connect to other articles using hyperlinked subject terms? Is there a "More Like This" feature or something similar?

7. Have the paraprofessional do a search using the advanced search feature.

8. If applicable, review related checklists "Federated Searching" and "Link Resolvers."

2. FEDERATED SEARCHING

OBJECTIVE

1. Be able to define federated searching.

Federated searching allows patrons to simultaneously search multiple databases, including the online catalog if desired, using a single interface. Not all individual database features will be available through federated searching. A goal of federated search is to simplify the search process.

If your library has implemented a federated search tool, consider the following checklist for training.

CHECKLIST

- Explain to the paraprofessional what federated searching is meant to achieve.
- For each type of search (e.g., basic, advanced), explain which databases are included in the search. For example:

Checking off the following category . . .	will search the following databases
Library Science	Academic Search Premier, Library Literature and Information Science Full Text, Library, Information Science, and Technology Abstracts and Research Library Complete
Biography	American National Biography, Biography Resource Center, and Biography Reference Bank

- It is also important to explain the differences between the search types; what fields are being searched (this will depend on local implementation of the federated search tool). For example:

Selecting the following search type . . .	searches the following database field(s)
Title	Title
Author	Author
Subject	Subject or Descriptor
Keyword	Title and subject
All	Author, Abstract, Subject, Title

- Have the employee run some searches using the federated search tool and then run the same search in the database's native interface. This exercise will allow the paraprofessional to see the similarities and differences in searching.

- The paraprofessional should be aware of what can and cannot be done using a federated search tool. For example, is it possible to limit to full text and/or peer-reviewed articles?

- Federated search results in a particular database can differ greatly from the results when using the databases' native interface. Point out that results might be presented in the order of retrieval (first come, first served) rather in order by relevancy.

- Have the paraprofessional observe what happens when he or she views the article. Does it open in a separate window? What happens if someone clicks on the hyperlinks in the article or tries to use the "More like this" feature? Is the search carried forward or does it reach a dead end? What options does the federated search tool provide for printing, saving, or e-mailing articles?

3. LINK RESOLVERS

OBJECTIVES

1. Be able to define what link resolvers do.
2. In any given database, locate the icon for the link resolver.
3. Using link resolvers, be able to determine whether the article is available in another database.

Link resolvers make it much easier for patrons to get to the full text of a desired article. For example, a patron searching in a general article database sees the abstract of an article that he or she wants, but there is no full text available. Without link resolvers, the patron would have to re-do the search in another database to see if the full text of the desired article were available in that resource. However, if the library has implemented link resolvers, the searcher can simply link to another database if the full text of the article is available in that database. In most cases, the user need only click on a link to see if the article is available elsewhere.

If your library uses a link resolver product, consider the following checklist for training.

CHECKLIST

- Explain to the paraprofessional what link resolving does.
- Have the employee run some searches in various databases that are not entirely full text to see what happens.
- Make sure the staff member can locate linking icons in each database. Examples include "Find a copy" and "Search for article."
- Demonstrate to the paraprofessional what happens in the browser when clicking on a linking icon. It is possible that the linking software opens into a separate browser window. In order to get back to the original search results, it might be necessary to click on the original window.
- Point out that, at times, the link resolver will not point to an article but to the journal that contains the article. The paraprofessional may have to "drill down" until he or she sees the volume and issue number of the journal that contains the article.

- If no electronic copy of the article is available, the library may subscribe to a print copy of the journal with the desired material. If the linking software provides the option to search the journal's ISSN in the library catalog, the paraprofessional should adopt the habit of doing so, especially if the journal title begins with "The."

- Finally, if no electronic or print copy is available at the library, the paraprofessional should understand how to assist in filling out an interlibrary loan request for the desired article.

4. SUPERINTENDENT OF DOCUMENTS (SUDOC) NUMBERS

OBJECTIVES

1. Understand how the Superintendent of Documents classification system arranges documents.
2. Be able to distinguish between a Library of Congress Classification number and a SuDoc number.
3. From memory, be able to put SuDoc numbers in order with no errors.

The Superintendent of Documents (SuDoc) classification system is used to arrange documents issued by various U.S. government agencies. The SuDoc numbers organize government documents by government agency, not by subject, as do the Library of Congress or Dewey Decimal System.

Because SuDoc numbers begin with letters and also use numbers, it can be easy to confuse them with Library of Congress numbers. The easiest way to recognize a SuDoc number is to look for the colon [:]. A call number with a colon indicates that the number is a SuDoc.

The first part of the SuDoc number indicates the cabinet or independent agency that issues the document. Below are some examples of SuDoc numbers and the corresponding agencies.

A	Department of Agriculture
C3	Census Bureau (Part of the Department of Commerce)
D	Defense Department
ED	Department of Education
HE	Department of Health and Human Services
J	Department of Justice
L	Department of Labor
PRex	Executive Office of the President
S	State Department
T22	Internal Revenue Service (Part of the Treasury Department)
Y	Congress
Y.4	Congressional Committees

Points to remember for SuDoc order:

- The numbers are arranged by the letter of the agency first.
- The number after the point is a whole number, not a decimal.
- If the call number is the same to a certain point, then varies, the proper order is: years, letters, numbers. For some years, the first number was dropped. Beginning with 2000, the years are comprised of four digits.
- If the number before the base number is followed by a slash and more numbers, the base number comes first, followed by the slashed numbers.

EXERCISE

Put the following SuDoc numbers in order.

Basic

a. C3.134/2:C83/2/2000

b. C3.134:2007

c. PREX 2.6/4:2002

d. ED1.140:2005

e. C3.134/5:2006

f. AE2.108/2:2006-2007

g. PREX 3.15:2006

h. J29.9/6:2003

i. PREX 2.6:IN 27/1987

j. L2.3/4:2006-1007

Advanced

a. D101.2: Se 2/5

b. D101.6/5: En 3/3

c. D101.6/5:C 76/2

d. D101.2: 96/2

e. D101.6/5:C 76/2/995

f. D101.6/5:C 76/2/1987

g. D101.2:P 94/11

h. D101.2.SE 6/992

i. D101.6/5:EN 3/4

j. D101.2: Sh 6

k. D101.6/5:C 76/2/2007

l. D101.2:SE 6/7

Answers
Basic: f, b, a, e, d, h, j, i, c, g,
Advanced: g, d, a, h, l, j, c, f, e, k, b, i

RESOURCES

FEDERATED SEARCHING

Cervone, Frank. 2007. "Federated Searching: Today, Tomorrow and the Future (?)." *Serials* 20, no. 1: 67–70. Cervone discusses the benefits of federated searching to patrons, features and trends, and some criticisms of this technology.

Tenopir, Carol. 2007. "Can Johnny Search?" *Library Journal* 132, no. 2 (February 1): 30. Tenopir discusses some criticisms of federated searching, such as loss of individual database features and lack of controlled vocabulary.

LINK RESOLVERS

Grogg, Jill E. 2006. "Introduction." *Library Technology Reports* 42, no. 1: 5–7. Jill Grogg writes extensively about link resolvers and linking software. The introduction to this volume of *Library Technology Reports,* which is entirely devoted to linking, provides the background to why linking software is useful.

Grogg, Jill E. 2006. "On the Road to the OpenURL." *Library Technology Reports* 42, no. 1: 8–13. Grogg provides definitions and examples of linking.

McDonald, John, and Eric F. Van de Velde. 2004. "The Lure of Linking." *Library Journal* 129, no. 6 (April 1): 32–34. McDonald and Van de Velde provide an overview of linking software.

SUDOC NUMBERS

"An Explanation of the Superintendent of Documents Classification System." Available: www.access.gpo.gov/su_docs/fdlp/pubs/explain.html. Accessed: June 15, 2008. The World Wide Web has numerous library guides and tutorials explaining the Superintendent of Documents classification system, which can be found using a search engine.

7 READY REFERENCE SKILLS

> Training modules for ready reference sources can be created by subject (company information, health information, etc.), type of resource (encyclopedias, directories, almanacs, etc.), or by a theme (holidays, History Fair, Science Fair, etc.).

This chapter presents modules that are meant to acquaint the paraprofessional with learning how to use basic reference tools; they are designed to instruct on how to use specific sources, not on how to answer the questions. There is a module for general encyclopedias and for a few subject areas. Frequently consulted ready reference resources, both print and electronic, are included. The sources in the modules are a subset of available reference sources and were selected using the following criteria:

1. Appeared in at least one of three library school texts: *Reference and Information Services* by Richard E. Bopp and Linda C. Smith; *Introduction to Reference Work: Basic Information Services,* Volume One by William A. Katz; and *Reference and Information Services in the 21st Century: An Introduction* by Kay Ann Cassell and Uma Hiremath.
2. Selected as appropriate for a paraprofessional.

As the paraprofessional becomes familiar with the tools at a particular location, he or she may find other ways to locate information (e.g., encyclopedia articles have information about foreign countries) to better locate information to these specific questions.

1. GENERAL ENCYCLOPEDIAS

OBJECTIVES

1. Understand the differences among the encyclopedias, including reading level and use of illustrations.
2. When using online encyclopedias, understand the differences between the different searching options offered.
3. When using print encyclopedias, use the index every time.

TRAINING HANDOUT

There are both generalized and specialized encyclopedias; this module focuses on general encyclopedias. General encyclopedias attempt to summarize a great deal of information about a great many topics.

Encyclopedias might contain detailed articles; shorter, explanatory material; and brief, factual data. Because of the variety of subjects covered and the depth of information that might be provided, an encyclopedia is a good source to use in the following instances:

- Supplying quick, factual answers. When did North Carolina become a state? Who wrote *The Magic Flute*? What is a photon?

- Providing general background and introductory information on a topic. Patrons may need to write a paper, and an encyclopedia article can provide important terms, dates, people, and concepts that will assist them in further research. Encyclopedia articles with bibliographies will also point patrons to other resources to consult on a particular topic.

Online encyclopedias have an advantage over print encyclopedias in that the content is usually updated frequently, and information can be retrieved via a search tool and is hyperlinked. The content often includes more than the articles; online encyclopedias have multimedia content, such as sound, animation, and videos. In addition, online encyclopedias often make other research tools, such as dictionaries, atlases, quotation tools, etc., available.

Print encyclopedias are arranged in alphabetical order, but one should always consult the index, as information about a certain topic might be contained in several entries. Because different encyclopedias have varying strengths and levels of complexity, it is important to learn about each one so that the appropriate resource is consulted.

World Book Online/World Book Encyclopedia

The target audience for *World Book Encyclopedia* is primary and secondary school students, yet it is a good reference tool for people of all ages. *World Book Encyclopedia* makes extensive use of color illustrations, tables, charts, and graphs.

> **Print Version:** Especially helpful in this version are the definitions of difficult words and phrases. An index is available.

> **Online Version:** This version has a basic search that fulfills most needs. The advanced search screen has options to perform Boolean searching, search by phrase, search for all words, search for any words, and to search by date. One can also search all content or pick and choose what to search (encyclopedia articles, maps, sounds, pictures, tables, dictionary, etc.). A browse function is also available.

Encyclopedia Americana/Encyclopedia America Online

In terms of sophistication, *Encyclopedia Americana* falls between *World Book* and *Encyclopedia Britannica*. It has shorter articles and is meant to "serve as the bridge between the specialist and the general reader." *Encyclopedia Americana* focuses on U.S. history, biography, and geography, but, as a general encyclopedia, it can be used for other subjects.

> **Print Version:** An index is available in this version.

> **Online Version:** This version has a basic search box where one can search either by article title or full text. Advanced search lets one perform Boolean searches, either of the article title or full text. A browse by subject function is also available.

Encyclopaedia Britannica Online/Encyclopaedia Britannica

The *Encyclopaedia Britannica* is geared to adults and is regarded as the most scholarly of general encyclopedias.

Print Version: The *Encyclopaedia Britannica* is comprised of three parts: the single-volume Propaedia, the twelve-volume Micropaedia, and the seventeen-volume Macropaedia. Reference queries will be answered using the Micropaedia and/or Macropaedia, as these volumes contain the articles; the Micropaedia has shorter entries, the Macropaedia, longer, more detailed material. The Propaedia is meant to be a guide to the contents of the Micropaedia and Macropaedia, but the best approach to locate information is to use the two-volume index.

Online Version: This version has a basic search box (standard search) and an advanced search. The advanced search allows one to search with all words, by exact phrase, with any words, without certain words, proximity searching, as well as the option to select content to search from

- *Encyclopaedia Britannica*
- *Britannica Concise*
- Multimedia
- Web sites

There is also the index, which is searchable and browseable, an "A-Z Browse" that one can search, a subject browse, a multimedia timeline, and a Year in Review Browse.

EXERCISE AND PRACTICE QUESTIONS

For each encyclopedia, read any information that provides details about the content or how to search. Explore the difference between all searching options. Practice browsing. Look at how the search results display. When clicking on an article or any other material, see what options are available to save, print, or export the information. For an article, does the entire article display or is it necessary to click on text such as "View Full Article" or "Contents" to get the full article?

Answer the practice questions below. Write down your search strategy.

For each encyclopedia, read the Preface or Introduction to understand the arrangement of the contents (alphabetization, index, cross-references, etc.), as well as to learn about special features of each encyclopedia. Then answer the following practice questions, which come from a variety of subjects (music, history, psychology, etc.), and will allow exploration of the differences among the three encyclopedias.

Practice Questions

1. What is Diwali and when is it celebrated?
2. I need to see the cross-section of a leaf.
3. I would like to see a time line of the Civil War.
4. Do you have a list of all the Heisman Trophy winners?
5. I need a good a good overview of Marxism.
6. I would like an explanation of Maslow's Hierarchy of Needs.
7. What is the difference between a major and minor scale?
8. I need pictures of the state flag, flower, and bird of Alabama.
9. What is Fool's Gold?
10. Where do Kurds live?

Answers to Practice Questions (Online)

1. a. *World Book Online:* **Search Strategy Used:** Type "diwali" into basic search box. The article is the first listed.

   b. *Encyclopedia Americana Online:* **Search Strategy Used:** Type "diwali" into search box with "article title" option selected. One article is retrieved.

   c. *Encyclopaedia Britannica Online:* **Search Strategy Used:** Type "diwali" into basic search box. The article is the first listed.

2. a. *World Book Online's* article "leaf" has a diagram, "Inside a typical green leaf." **Search Strategy Used:** Type "leaf" into basic search box.

   b. *Encyclopedia Americana Online's* article "leaf" has a diagram, "Structure of a Typical Leaf." **Search Strategy Used:** Type "leaf" into search box with "article title" option selected.

   c. *Encyclopaedia Britannica Online:* The article leaf has images, one of which is an illustration, "leaf cellular structure." **Search Strategy Used:** Type "leaf" in standard search box; the first article is "Leaf." Click on "Images" for the article leaf. Another search strategy is to type "cross-section of a leaf" in standard search box. The result under "media" has the desired picture.

3. a. *World Book Online* provides time lines in many of its articles and the article "Civil War, American" includes a table, "Important events during the American Civil War," that provides events and dates at a glance. **Search Strategy Used:** Type "civil war" into basic search box. "Civil War, American" is the first search result.

   b. *Encyclopedia Americana Online:* Has an article "Civil War" but no time line. In the article section "Appended material" there is information, "Important Battles of the Civil War." **Search Strategy Used:** Type "civil war" into search box with "article title" option selected. The article "Civil War" is the ninth article listed. Click on "Contents" to get all the article sections listed.

   c. *Encyclopaedia Britannica Online's* article "American Civil War" does not have an actual time line. The interactive time lines do not have a time line of the Civil War. **Search Strategy Used:** Typing "civil war" in standard search box yields many articles; "American Civil War" is the sixth article.

4. a. *World Book Online* has an article, "Heisman Memorial Trophy." The article text states that a list of trophy winners is included in the article "Football," which is linked. It is necessary to view the entire article "Football" in order to see the link to "Heisman Trophy Winners." **Search Strategy Used:** Type "heisman" into basic search box. "Heisman Memorial Trophy" is the first search result.

   b. *Encyclopedia Americana Online* does not have an article about the Heisman trophy but it is possible to find this information in the article "Football." **Search Strategy Used:** Typing "heisman" into basic search box gets no results. Type "heisman" into basic search box with option for "full text" selected. Fourth search result is the appended material for football. Click on the link, then click on contents; the appended material includes a list of Heisman Trophy winners.

   c. *Encyclopaedia Britannica Online's* article about the trophy does not include a list of winners. **Search Strategy Used:** Typing "heisman" into standard search box pulls up the article "Heisman Trophy."

5. a. *World Book Online* has information about Marxism under the article "Marx, Karl." **Search Strategy Used:** Type "marxism" into basic search box. "Marx, Karl" is the fifteenth article in the list.

   b. *Encyclopedia Americana Online* has an article titled "Marxism." **Search Strategy Used:** Type "marxism" into search box with "article title" option selected. This retrieves the article "Marxism."

   c. *Encyclopaedia Britannica Online* has a lengthy article on Marxism, as well as information about Marxism embedded in other articles (e.g. "religion, philosophy of " article). **Search Strategy Used:** Type "marxism" into standard search box pulls up the article "Marxism" along with many other articles.

6. a. *World Book Online* has the information in article "Maslow, Abraham Harold." **Search Strategy Used:** Tying in "hierarchy of needs" in both the basic and advanced search boxes got no results. Typing in "maslow" in the basic search box retrieves the article "Maslow, Abraham Harold."

   b. *Encyclopedia Americana Online* has the information in the article "Motivation." **Search Strategy Used:** Typing "hierarchy of needs" into search box with "article title" option selected yields no results. Typing "hierarchy of needs" into search box with "full text" option selected retrieves the article "Motivation."

   c. *Encyclopaedia Britannica Online* can be found in the article "Maslow, Abraham H." as well as in the articles "Self," "Motivation" (in the "Self-actualization" section), and "Humanistic Psychology." **Search Strategy Used:** Type "hierarchy of needs" into standard search box. The first article is "Self"; "Maslow, Abraham H." is second.

7. a. *World Book Online:* The article "Music" explains the difference in the section "Tone." **Search Strategy Used:** Type "major scale" into the basic search box. "Music" is the second article.

   b. *Encyclopedia Americana Online:* The article "Scale" explains the difference. **Search Strategy Used:** Typing in "major scale" into the basic search gets no results. Switch the search to "full text" and "Scale" is the first article in the list.

c. *Encyclopaedia Britannica Online* has an article for "Major Scale" and an article for "Minor Scale." The article "Scale" also has information on major and minor scales. **Search Strategy Used:** In the standard search box, type in "major scale" and "minor scale," respectively. To get the article "Scale," type in standard search box word "scale"; the section "common scale types" has the explanation.

8. a. *World Book Online's* article "Alabama" has pictures of the state flag, seal, bird, flower, and tree. **Search Strategy Used:** Type "alabama flag" into the basic search box. Search results include a picture "Alabama flag and seal" which is part of the larger article "Alabama"; this article contains the picture mentioned above, along with the picture "Alabama bird, flower, and tree."

b. *Encyclopedia Americana Online:* There is only a picture of the flag, although it is possible to find out the names of the state bird, flower, and tree. **Search Strategy Used:** Using the term "alabama" in the standard search box, it is possible to find this information clicking on the "Tables" link under "Content Related to this Topic," "State nicknames and symbols."

c. *Encyclopedia Americana Online* has this information (but without pictures) in the article "Alabama" under the section "Appended Material." **Search Strategy Used:** Type in "alabama" into search box with "article title" option selected. The fifth article is "Alabama." Click on "Contents" to get links to all articles sections.

9. a. *World Book Online:* **Search Strategy Used:** Type "fool's gold" into the basic search box. The single result is the article "Pyrite."

b. *Encyclopedia Americana Online:* **Search Strategy Used:** Typing "fool's gold" into search box with "article title" option selected yields no results. Type "fool's gold" into search box with "full text" option selected retrieves six articles, including the articles "Chalcopyrite" and "Pyrite."

c. *Encyclopaedia Britannica Online:* **Search Strategy Used:** Type "fool's gold" into Standard Search box. The first article is "pyrite."

10. a. *World Book Online's* article "Kurds" clearly states where the Kurds live and provides a map, "Kurds' homeland area." **Search Strategy Used:** Type "kurds" into the basic search box. "Kurds" is the first article in the list.

b. *Encyclopedia Americana Online's* article "Kurd" provides information on where the Kurds live. **Search Strategy Used:** Typing "kurds" into search box with "article title" option selected yields no results. Type "kurd" into search box with "full text" option selected retrieves the article "Kurd."

c. *Encyclopaedia Britannica Online:* The article "Kurd" and the "Kurds" portion of "Iraq" article answer this question, and the results under "Media" show a map of "Kurd: areas of majority Kurdish settlement." **Search Strategy Used:** Type "kurds" into standard search box. The first two articles are "Kurd" and "Kurds."

Answers to Practice Questions (Print)

1. All three encyclopedias have information on Diwali, the Hindu festival of lights. *Encyclopedia Americana's* entry best answers the question, listing what the festival celebrates and clearly stating Diwali is celebrated in October and November. The *Encyclopaedia Britannica* has a Micropaedia article on Diwali; Diwali is also mentioned in the Macropaedia articles on India and Hinduism. *Encyclopaedia Britannica's* article on Diwali is less clear when the festival takes place. *World Book Encyclopedia's* index points the reader to the article "Feasts and Festivals" which provides brief information about Diwali but does not state when Diwali occurs.

2. Both *World Book Encyclopedia* and *Encyclopedia Americana* have pictures of a leaf's cross-section. The diagram in *World Book Encyclopedia* is in color with more detail, showing the section in relation to the leaf and providing pictures of open and closed guard cells. *Encyclopaedia Britannica* has no such diagram, although it provides textual information about leaves.

3. *World Book Encyclopedia* provides time lines in many of its articles, including in the article "Civil War,

American." "Important events during the American Civil War" provides events and dates at a glance. None of the articles in *Encyclopedia Americana* or *Encyclopaedia Britannica* have actual time lines.

4. This question can be answered using both *World Book Encyclopedia* and *Encyclopedia Americana*. *Encyclopedia Britannica's* article about the trophy does not include a list of winners.

5. The most in-depth article is the *Encyclopaedia Britannica's* Macropedia article "Marx and Marxism," which is twelve pages and provides biographical information on Marx, Marxism, Russian and Soviet Marxism, and other variants of Marxism. There is also a Micropaedia article. *World Book Encyclopedia* has a briefer article and *Encyclopedia Americana's* article falls in the middle.

6. *Encyclopaedia Britannica's* index has several entries under the name "Maslow, Abraham Harold," including one for "human hierarchy of needs." This material can be found in the article "Humanistic Psychology." In the case of *Encyclopaedia Britannica,* it is worthwhile to look at all index entries, for the most complete information can be found in the Macropedia article "Motivation." Although it is not obvious from the index, it is possible to find this information in *World Book Encyclopedia's* article on Maslow. *Encyclopedia Americana's* index has several entries for Maslow but only the article "Educational Psychology" has any information on needs.

7. It is easiest to find this information in the *World Book Encyclopedia,* which has index entries for both "Major scale" and "Minor scale" pointing to the article "Music (Tone)." This article explains the distinction between the two scales and provides diagrams. *Encyclopedia Americana* has an index entry for minor scale but not major scale; however, the article "minor" does explain the difference. *Encyclopedia Americana's* index also has an entry for "Scale (music)," which point to articles with more in-depth information. *Encyclopaedia Britannica* has index entries for major and minor scales, which lead to a brief treatment in the Micropaedia under "scale" and a fuller one in the Macropaedia under "Music, the Art of."

8. *World Book Encyclopedia's* article on Alabama has a section "Symbols of Alabama" with pictures of the state flag, seal, bird, flower, and tree. *Encyclopedia Americana* provides information on the state bird, nickname, etc., but without pictures. *Encyclopaedia Britannica* has a table with this information for each state, but no pictures.

9. Both indexes for *World Book Encyclopedia* and *Encyclopaedia Britannica* refer the reader to pyrite, but *Encyclopedia Americana's* index points the user to both pyrite and chalcopyrite.

10. All three encyclopedias indexes have entries for either "Kurd" or "Kurds." *World Book Encyclopedia* and *Encyclopedia Americana* clearly state where the Kurds live and provide a map; *Encyclopedia Americana's* map is larger and the article "Kurdistan" following "Kurd" is also very helpful. *Encyclopedia Britannica's* Micropaedia article has two statements regarding where Kurds live; one sentence is about where most Kurds live, and the other refers to communities of Kurds.

A NOTE ABOUT WIKIPEDIA

Wikipedia is one of the top information resources in the world; 36 percent of Americans turn to it regularly. It is current, has an amazing amount of information, and is easy to use. Yet, the lack of editors, falsified entries, and the fact that anyone can contribute to Wikipedia has spawned a great deal of controversy in libraries.

The supervisor should discuss whether it is acceptable in the reference department for the paraprofessional to consult Wikipedia. There may be certain subjects for which the supervisor considers it unacceptable to consult this source. Either way, the supervisor should point out the pitfalls of Wikipedia, the lack of "authority," the potential for hoaxes, etc. If permissible for the paraprofessional, it is wise to have the paraprofessional run some searches in Wikipedia to compare to the traditional encyclopedias. A good exercise could be to combine the exercises from this module together with the exercise in Chapter 5.

2. INTERNATIONAL INFORMATION

OBJECTIVES

1. Be familiar with how each resource has the information on countries arranged.
2. Using any resources available, correctly answer 90 percent of all questions about countries of the world and international organizations.

TRAINING HANDOUT

Patrons ask for information about other countries for a variety of reasons. The patron might be writing a report for school, preparing to travel abroad, satisfying curiosity, etc. Depending on the question, the library has numerous sources that can help. Three frequently consulted general reference sources, each available either electronically or in print, are listed below.

The Statesman's Yearbook: The Politics, Cultures, and Economies of the World

This reference work (also available electronically via subscription) provides information on the countries of the world and on international organizations. A typical entry for a country provides information on key historical events, territory and population, recent elections, current administration, international relations, economy, energy and natural resources, industry, international trade, communications, social institutions, and culture. Suggestions for further reading are provided.

> **Print only:** Two indexes, "Current Leaders Index," and "Place and International Organizations Index" are available.

The Europa World Year Book

The Europa World Year Book (also available electronically via subscription) provides details on the political, economic, and commercial institutions of the world. Extensive coverage is provided for over 1000 international organizations, including the United Nations and related agencies. Following the section on international organizations are chapters devoted to each country of the world. These chapters contain a great deal of information, including recent history, economics, defense, statistics, and a directory section. The "Introductory Survey" for each nation provides an excellent overview.

> **Print only:** There is a small index of territories at the end of Volume Two.

CIA World Factbook

The CIA World Factbook (available on the Internet at www.cia.gov/library/publications/the-world-factbook/index.html), which has its origins in the Central Intelligence Agency's intelligence-gathering process, provides only very brief information on countries and international organizations; both *The Stateman's Yearbook* and *The Europa World Year Book* provide far more in-depth information. Yet, this source should not be overlooked, as it does provide some unique information, and most importantly, is available for free on the Internet. This resource provides maps, information on a country's geography, peoples, government, economy, and communications.

PRACTICE QUESTIONS

1. What holidays do people celebrate in France?
2. What is the name of the national anthem for South Africa?
3. Can I get a list of newspapers published in China?
4. What are the ethnic groups in Afghanistan?
5. What international organizations is Turkey a member of?
6. Does Lithuania have a VAT (value-added tax)?
7. What religions do people practice in Malaysia?
8. I need information about India's armed forces.
9. I need an overview of the League of Arab States.
10. What is the Internet code for Georgia?

Answers to Practice Questions

1. *The CIA World Factbook* lists only one national holiday: Bastille Day, which falls on July 14. *The Statesman's Yearbook* does not have an evident list of

holidays, but in the section "Festivals" the portion "Religious Festivals" states that the Assumption of the Blessed Virgin Mary and All Saints Day are both public holidays. *The Europa World Year Book* provides the most comprehensive list under "Public Holidays": New Year's Day, Easter Monday, Labor Day, Ascension Day, Liberation Day, National Day, Fall of the Bastille, Assumption, All Saints' Day, Armistice Day, and Christmas Day.

2. *The Statesman's Yearbook,* in the section "Constitution and Government," subsection "National Anthem" states the national anthem is "is a combination of shortened forms of "Die Stem van Suid-Afrika"/"The Call of South Africa" and "Nkosi Sikelel' iAfrika"/"God bless Africa." Neither *The Europa World Year Book* nor *The CIA World Factbook* supplies this information.

3. *The Stateman's Yearbook's* general description of the Chinese press contains the names of two newspapers: *Renmin Ribao* and *Sichauan Ribao. The Europa World Year Book* lists over 50 "principal" newspapers, including addresses for some. *The CIA World Factbook* does not provide any names of newspapers.

4. This question can be answered using either the *The Statesman's Yearbook* and or *The CIA World Factbook; The Stateman's Yearbook* lists Pashtuns, Tajiks, Hazaras, and Uzbeks, while *The CIA World Factbook* additionally lists the Aiman, the Turkmen, and the Baloch. *The Europa World Year Book* is not the source to consult for this information.

5. It is very easy to locate this information in *The CIA World Factbook;* there is a section "International organization participation" containing a list of over 60 acronyms of organizations (Appendix A "Abbreviations" spells out the abbreviations while Appendix B "International Organizations and Groups" provides more information on the organizations.). A much smaller listing can be found in *The Statesman's Yearbook* under "International Relations." It is possible to glean this information in *The Europa World Year Book,* but the information is scattered among the various sections in the Introductory Survey.

6. Under Economy—Budget, *The Statesman's Yearbook* states that the VAT is 18 percent, with reduced rates of 9 and 5 percent. Neither *The CIA World Factbook* nor *The Europa World Year Book* provides this information.

7. All three sources can provide this information, but *The Statesman's Yearbook* provides the most names: Islam, Buddhism, Taoism, Hinduism and Christianity. The CIA World Factbook simply lists "Muslim, indigenous beliefs, Christianity"; *The Europa World Year Book* lists Islam, Buddhism, Hinduism, Christianity, and "traditional beliefs" in the introductory survey's section "Location, Climate, Language, Religion, Flag, Capital." In the "Directory" portion, there is information on religious leaders, organizations and institutions.

8. Each source has something about India's military, but the scope varies. *The Statesman's Yearbook,* under "Defence," presents a narrative and descriptions, along with facts and figures. *The CIA World Factbook* lists branches of the military, along with some statistics (expenditure, manpower, etc.). *The Europa World Year Book* gives numbers on manpower and budget information.

9. *The CIA World Factbook* provides information only on date of establishment, aim, and membership. *The Statesman's Yearbook* provides more details on the origin and membership, as well as information on joint action, the Arab Common Market, the organization, and a Web site. *The Europa World Year Book* gives the best overview, with a multipage treatment, including council, secretariat, specialized agencies, addresses of Arab League offices, and activities related to security, water resources, Arab-Israeli affairs, conflict in the Persian Gulf, and more.

10. *The CIA World Factbook* lists the Internet country code as .ge. Neither *The Statesman's Yearbook* nor *The Europa World Year Book* supplies an answer to this question.

3. STATISTICS

OBJECTIVES

1. Using any resources available, identify the library's sources on statistics.
2. Using any statistical resource, consult the index each time.

TRAINING HANDOUT

Statistics come from many sources, such as the federal government (most notably the Census Bureau), but also from state and foreign governments, international organizations, nonprofits, and private industry. Depending what is being requested, the difficulty in finding statistics will vary. In some cases, particular statistics may not exist or may not be publicly available. For example, the government publishes statistics about categories of people and businesses, but, due to privacy concerns, not about individual persons or businesses. It is also important to note that the frequency of data collection for statistics may vary; for example, the Census count for population and housing is only conducted every ten years; the Economic Census, every five years. Therefore the most recent statistic available might be up to several years old.

The best place to begin looking for statistics is to consult one or more of the four sources described below. Each resource has an index, which you should use to help you determine whether you can find the statistic.

Statistical Abstract of the United States

The first place to look for most statistics will be the *Statistical Abstract of the United States* (Washington, DC: U.S. Census Bureau. Annual; available on the Internet at http://www.census.gov/compendia/statab/). The *Statistical Abstract* is a one-volume summary of the social, political, and economic organization of the United States. The *Statistical Abstract* pulls together data from both government and private sources. Generally, the emphasis is placed on national data but some tables provide data on the regional, state, metropolitan area, and city levels. Sometimes international data will be included. It is important to note that the statistics may not be up to date; statistics are for the most recent year available or for the period available for the summer of the prior year (e.g., June 2006 for the 2007 *Statistical Abstract*). For further information on statistics in the *Statistical Abstract,* each table includes a source note that lists the source for the original data.

The World Almanac and Book of Facts

The World Almanac and Book of Facts (New York: World Almanac Books. Annual) provides succinct factual information about a variety of topics, including some statistics. *The World Almanac* often uses the same statistical sources as the *Statistical Abstract* but presents the data differently, sometimes in more detail. For that reason, this work should be consulted when trying to locate statistics. There are several indexes; when checking this resource for statistics, be sure to use the more detailed General Index as opposed to the more general Quick Reference Index.

County and City Data Book: 2000

The *County and City Data Book* (Washington, DC: United States Census Bureau. Irregular; available on the Internet at www.census.gov/prod/www/abs/ccdb07.html) provides summary statistics on the social and economic structure of cities and counties and is meant to be a supplement to the *Statistical Abstract of the United States.* And while the emphasis is on data for counties and cities, there is some state and national information, as well as population data for places and minor civil divisions (MCDs) with more than 2,500 inhabitants. The Preface provides greater details on how the Census Bureau defines a "city" and "place." There are four categories of tables "States" "Counties," "Cities of 25,000 or More Population," and "Places/MCDs of 2500 or More Population." The subject guide, which serves as the index, can help determine whether particular data are available.

Statistical Yearbook

The United Nations' *Statistical Yearbook* (New York: United Nations, Statistical Office. Annual) is the international equivalent to the *Statistical Abstract.* This work provides a wide range of statistics, on an international level, on social and economic conditions. There is an index to guide one to the appropriate table(s).

PRACTICE QUESTIONS

1. I need a list of SAT scores by state.
2. How many hazardous waste sites are in the United States?
3. What is the racial makeup of Los Angeles County?
4. I need statistics of traffic fatalities for the states.

5. What is the population of Cullowhee, North Carolina?

6. I want statistics on U.S. foreign aid to Africa.

7. I need to get numbers on what languages besides English are spoken in the United States.

8. I want to compare the production and consumption of meat between the United States and the European Union.

9. I need information on numbers of cell phones and telephone lines throughout the world.

10. Who emits more CFCs? China? Or the United States?

Answers to Practice Questions

1. Consult the General Index of *The World Almanac* under "Scholastic Aptitude Testing (SAT) Program." *World Almanac* provides a breakdown of SAT mean scores by state, for both verbal and math scores. The index of the *Statistical Abstract* provides a table of "SAT Scores and Characteristics of College-Bound Seniors" but does not provide state-by-state information. Both *The World Almanac* and the *Statistical Abstract* cite The College Board as the source for their statistics.

2. The general index "Hazardous Waste Sites" in *The World Almanac* has a breakdown of hazardous waste sites by state, along with the number of proposed and final (qualified for Superfund financing) and how many of the proposed and final are federal and non federal sites. This information is current as of 2006. The information in the *Statistical Abstract* is current as of 2004 but provides rankings. Both sources cite the Environmental Protection Agency.

3. *County and City Data Book* is a clear choice for information about counties. There is a table "Counties—Population by Age, Sex, and Race," which provides racial breakdowns for each county, state by state.

4. Neither the *Statistical Yearbook* nor *The County and City Data Book* provides this information. *The World Almanac* has statistics on general motor vehicle accidents, but not broken down by state. *Statistical Abstract* has a table, "Traffic Fatalities by State."

5. This can be found in *The County and City Data Book* under "Places—Area and Population;" it is not under "Cities—Area and Population." To find Cullowhee, it is necessary to go to "North Carolina" then look for Cullowhee. Because the *Statistical Abstract* places emphasis on national level data, this is too minute to be included; this statistic is also beyond the scope of *The World Almanac* and *Statistical Yearbook*.

6. Since the *County and City Data Book* focuses on data for U.S. cities and counties, this is not the source to consult. *The World Almanac* does have an index entry for "Foreign aid" but only provides information on the amount of aid given by the United States, as well as the top ten recipients of U.S. development aid. The *Statistical Abstract* lists several tables in its index under "Foreign aid or assistance." One of those tables provides details of U.S. Foreign and Military Aid by Major Recipient Country. The patron would have to determine whether all African nations are represented in the list and proceed from that point. Another table (not referenced under the entry "Foreign aid or assistance" but sandwiched between two tables that are mentioned) lists total aid for "Middle East and North Africa" and "Sub-Saharan Africa." This particular table is reference under "Foreign countries—Aid to developing countries." It is important to check more than one place in the index.

7. Both *The World Almanac* and *Statistical Abstract* provide these data, although the *Statistical Abstract* has more current information. *The World Almanac's* numbers are from the year 2000 (source is the 2000 Census) and only lists 27 languages. The *Statistical Abstract* provides data from the Census Bureau's 2004 American Community Survey for 39 languages. Both tables are easily located in each work's respective index under "Language—Spoken in U.S. homes" and "Languages spoken at home."

8. Though it has index entries for "Meat—Consumption" and "Meat—Production," *The World Almanac* gives statistics only for the United States. The 2007 *Statistical Abstract* has the tables "Meat Production by Type and Country: 2003 to 2004" and "Meat Consumption by Type and Country: 2004 to 2005." A slight drawback is that the production figures for 2004 are

preliminary. The *Statistical Yearbook* provides a very comprehensive breakdown of meat production. The figures for 2004 are not preliminary; in addition numbers for each European country, along with Europe as a whole, are provided. There are no tables for meat consumption. This is an instance where two sources should be used.

9. *The World Almanac,* the *Statistical Yearbook,* and the *Statistical Abstract* all provide some sort of statistics on cell phones. The *World Almanac* provides a table on "World Wide Use of Cellular Telephones, Year—End 2005"; The *Statistical Abstract* has a small table "Telephones and Computers by Country: 2004," which includes data on telephone main lines and cellular phone subscribers for 37 nations. *The World Almanac* lists more countries, 62, but fails to supply information on land lines. The *Statistical Yearbook* has two very comprehensive tables "Cellular mobile telephone subscribers" and "Telephones—Main telephone lines in operation and lines per 100 inhabitants," and these provide data for the greatest number of countries. All three sources rely on data from the International Telecommunication Union (ITU) for their information.

10. CFCs stand for chlorofluorocarbons; scanning the index to *Statistical Yearbook,* there is an entry for chloroflurocarbon (CFC) consumption. The latest data for China and the United States are for the year 2004. *The World Almanac* provides good information on the greenhouse effect and global warming, but only gives comparisons for carbon dioxide emissions.

4. GOVERNMENT INDIVIDUALS AND AGENCIES

OBJECTIVES

1. Using any resources available, identify directories of individuals in government.
2. Using any resources available, identify information sources about government agencies and government activities.
3. Be familiar with the Web sites: www.house.gov and www.senate.gov.
4. Using any resources available, correctly answer 90 percent of all questions about individuals in government, government agencies, and government activities.

TRAINING HANDOUT

For questions about individuals in government, government agencies, services, and activities, it is possible to provide answers using both print and electronic sources. An advantage to the Internet is that the information found there is likely to be more up to date and can be accessed via a search engine. A disadvantage is that the search results can be enormous and time-consuming to navigate, whereas it can sometimes be faster to locate information in a print resource. Also, in the case of biographical information about individuals, print resources present the information in a consistent, uniform manner; in the case of an individual's Web site (e.g., senators and representatives), it is that individual's discretion s to what information appears and where.

Federal Yellow Book

The *Federal Yellow Book* (also available electronically via subscription) gives names, titles, telephone numbers, and addresses of employees in the Executive Office of the President, Office of the Vice President, departments, and independent agencies.

> **Print only:** There are three indexes: subject, name, and organization.

Federal Staff Directory

The *Federal Staff Directory* (also available electronically via subscription) lists the offices of the federal government. This work is comprised of five sections: Executive Office of the President, cabinet-level departments, independent agencies, and quasi-official, international, and nongovernment organizations, and executive biographies. Subject and individual indexes are available.

Politics in America

Each state profile in *Politics in America* (also available electronically via subscription) includes information on governors, state legislatures, and major cities. Profiles for senators and representatives contain basic biographical information (religion, education, hometown, etc.) and an essay. Ratings by four advocacy groups for each member appear at the end of each profile.

> **Print only:** Arranged alphabetically by state.

Congressional Yellow Book

This reference source (also available electronically via subscription) provides names, contact information, biographical information, a listing of staff aides, state and district offices, and leadership and member organizations for members of Congress. There are also sections on Senate, House, and joint committees. Indexes for name, subject and jurisdiction, and organization are available.

The United States Government Manual

The United States Government Manual (Washington, DC: Government Printing Office: Office of the Federal Register. Annual; available on the Internet at www.gpoaccess.gov/gmanual/index.html) serves as the official guide of the U.S. federal government. It provides information on the legislative, judicial, and executive branches of government, as well as details on quasi-official agencies, international organizations in which the United States takes part, commissions, and committees. Agency descriptions include a list of primary officials, summary of its purpose and role in government, and a description of its activities.

Government Web Sites

The Web sites www.house.gov and www.senate.gov are the official Web sites of the House of Representatives and the Senate, respectively. These sites provide information on members, such as voting records, individual Web sites, and committees. Each site provides various tools such as name search, state search, and tools to find bills, amendments, and debates.

PRACTICE QUESTIONS

1. I need an organization chart for the Department of Defense.
2. What zip codes does the 9th Congressional District cover?
3. I want to know the religion of Representative Jesse Jackson Jr.
4. I need to know who is on the Senate Armed Services Committee.
5. I've just moved and I have no idea who my representative is.
6. Are there any federal agencies that deal with homelessness?
7. I need a list of mailing and e-mail addresses for the presidential libraries.
8. What does the Chairman of the Joint Chiefs of Staff do?
9. Which members of Congress have served in the military?
10. I want to know how my representative voted on several issues.

Answers to Practice Questions

1. *The United States Government Manual* and *The Federal Staff Directory* have organization charts for government agencies. Simply go to the section of the manual that deals with that agency.
2. *The Congressional Yellow Book* has maps of districts along with zip codes by congressional districts.

3. This information is easily found in the congressional member's profiles in both the *Congressional Yellow Book* and *Politics in America*.

4. The Senate Web site, www.senate.gov, will have the most up-to-date information. There is a link to committees on the Web site, as well as a search box. Searching "Senate Armed Services Committee" using a search engine should also retrieve this information.

5. The House of Representative Web site, www.house.gov, has a search engine that lets one plug in a zip code. Results provide the name of the representative, along with a link to a Web page, along with the district number.

6. The subject index to *Federal Yellow Book* has an entry for "Homelessness" and has an entry for Interagency Council on Homelessness, which "coordinates the federal response to homelessness." The other entry is "Office of Homeless Veterans Programs," which is part of the Department of Veterans Affairs.

7. The *U.S. Government Manual* has a list of mailing addresses but provides no e-mail addresses. Both the *Federal Yellow Book* and the *Federal Staff Directory* provide this information. The *Federal Yellow Book* provides a more detailed staff listing than does the *Federal Staff Directory*.

8. The *United States Government Manual* has some information about the Chairman of the Joint Chiefs, but *Federal Staff Directory* provides greater detail on that position's duties.

9. *Politics in America* has a section "Member Statistics" that includes a list of all senators and representatives who have served in the military.

10. *Politics in America* provides key votes for the two previous years. www.house.gov also provides roll call votes.

5. COMPANY INFORMATION

OBJECTIVES

1. Understand the difference between a parent and a subsidiary.
2. Be able to distinguish between a public and a private company.
3. Be able to search using the "Companies" search tab in Hoover's Premium and the "Company" search option in Business and Company Resource Center.
4. Using any resources available, correctly answer 90 percent of all questions about company information.

TRAINING HANDOUT

Libraries often receive requests for information about companies and businesses. Requests are made to write a letter of complaint, to generate a list of sales leads or prospective employers, to explore investing in that company, or to find out who provides a particular service or manufactures a specific product.

Gather some basic information about the company during the reference interview. What does the company do? Is it a public or private company? Where is the company located? What else can you tell me about the company? Finding out as much as possible will allow you to match the patron information need with the appropriate resources.

It is important for the paraprofessional to have some basic knowledge about doing company research. A primary issue is knowing the difference between a public and private company.

- *Private companies* are owned by an individual, family, or group of partners. The amount of information that private companies must report is limited, and much of that is confidential. Thus, it is often difficult to find much information on a private company
- *Public companies* issue securities or shares of stock for the public, a process that is regulated by the Securities and Exchange Commission (SEC). Consequently, public companies are required to file numerous financial and other reports with the SEC. Because these reports are public information, it is easy to research public companies. An easy way to tell if a company is public is the presence of a ticker symbol.

Paraprofessionals should understand the difference between a parent company and a subsidiary. A subsidiary is a company that is owned by another company, or the parent company. In order to get information about a subsidiary, it may be necessary to research the parent company.

The paraprofessional should also be aware that a company's popular name may not be its official name. For example, United Airlines is a popular name but its real name is UAL Corporation; Walgreen's is the Walgreen Company.

Numerous sources provide information about a company. However, it is important to realize that not all the sources are the same. Knowing the nuances will help get the right information. The list below includes two of the most frequently consulted electronic resources in day-to-day general reference work as well as three very common print resources.

Hoover's Premium

Hoover's Premium (online) provides in-depth profiles of approximately 15,000 public and private companies in the United States and the world. Profiles include a basic fact sheet about the company, a highly readable overview about the company, a list of products and operations, names of competitors, people (company officers and employees), links to news stories, and financial data. Although several search options are available, the exercises here use only the choice "companies."

Business and Company Resource Center

Business and Company Resource Center (online) is a powerful resource that allows one to search for company profiles, company histories, industry surveys, and articles from business periodicals. This module will focus solely on searching for companies. It is best to always click on the "Company" icon under "Additional Search Options." This search feature lets one search by the company name, symbol, product/brand name, product/brand type, city, and state or country and more.

The results under "Company Search" are broken out into tabs: Company Profile, News/Magazines, Histories, Investment Reports, Financials, Rankings, Suits and Claims, Products, Industry Overviews, and Associations. If there is no information for a particular category, the tab is grayed out.

Standard & Poor's Register of Corporations, Directors, and Executives

This work (McGraw-Hill Companies, Inc.) is in two volumes. The first volume is in alphabetical order by business name. Company listings include address, telephone number, ticker symbol, information on principals of the companies, names (when available) of the company's primary accounting, bank and law firms, description of the company's products and services. Volume Two contains the listings of individuals (directors and executives) as well as the indices, which include a geographical index, cross-reference Index, and ultimate parent index. It is also important to be familiar with the "Key to Abbreviations" for this resource. The publisher also issues interim supplements to keep track of changes that have occurred since the publication of the annual volume.

LexisNexis Corporate Affiliations

Also known as "Who owns whom," this multivolume tool (LexisNexis, annual; also available electronically via subscription) covers "major public and private" businesses both in the United States and worldwide. Criteria for inclusion are "flexible" but in general, U.S. companies must have a revenue in excess of over $10 million, a workforce exceeding 300 persons, or be traded on a major stock exchange. Non-U.S. companies must have revenues of over $10 million.

This set is divided into the Master Index, U.S. Public Companies, U.S. Private Companies, and International Public and Private Companies; the latter three categories contain the information on the companies. Because companies are not listed alphabetically in a single volume, it is important to always use the master index when researching a company. Within the company listings, the information is organized by the parent company and by hierarchy; no matter where a subsidiary is located, it will be found in the same volume as the parent. Because corporate reporting can be very confusing, it is important to read "How to Use *Corporate Affiliations.*" Especially helpful is the "Understanding Levels of Reportage." In addition, the parts of the sets with company listings also have a section on use.

Million Dollar Directory

To be included in the *Million Dollar Directory* (Dun & Bradstreet; also available electronically via subscription), a company must meet one of two criteria: there must be more than $9,000,000 in sales volume *or* the company must be of a certain size. This resource contains information on both public and private companies. The primary listings for the businesses are in alphabetical order, with geographical and SIC indexes. In addition to address and phone number, the listings include information (when available) on annual sales, number of employees, company officers, board of directors, founding date, banking and accounting relationships, and more. Especially helpful is the section "Understanding Standard Industrial Classification (SIC) Codes" and the glossary.

EXERCISE

Take a well-known company (e.g., Starbucks) and compare how it is covered in all the sources. For the print sources, pay attention to the indices and how one can locate information. Similarly, for the online sources, pay attention to the search options; what kind of search terms can you use to locate information? Do the same for a lesser-known company, perhaps one that is small and local.

PRACTICE QUESTIONS

1. Who are Boeing's competitors?
2. Who makes Thunderbird wine?
3. I need to know the ticker symbol for Apple Computer, what stock exchange it is traded on, and Apple's transfer agent.
4. Who owns Old Navy?
5. I need sales figures for the Mars Company.
6. I would like to know who is on the board of directors for Halliburton.
7. I would like to contact the person in charge of Asheville Waste Paper.
8. Is Ford Motor Company involved in any joint ventures?

Answers to Practice Questions

1. Under the "Competitors" link, Hoover's Premium provides both top competitors and all competitors. It is possible to find this information in Business and Company Resource Center, but one must click on the "Industry Overview" tab which has a link to the article on aircraft in the online edition of Encyclopedia of Global Industries; this article discusses other aircraft manufacturers in addition to Boeing. *LexisNexis Corporate Affiliations,* the *Million Dollar Directory,* and *Standard and Poor's Register* do not provide a list of competitors.

2. Hoover's Premium provides the answer. It is best to type in both terms "thunderbird" and "wine" in the search box to get the result; "thunderbird" alone produces too many results. The only result is E & J Gallo

Winery. It is possible to see Thunderbird, along with other labels, under "Products/Operations." In the Full Overview, under History, the narrative states that E & J Gallo Winery introduced Thunderbird in 1957. The way the question is phrased, it is not possible to find this information in *Standard & Poor's Register,* the *Million Dollar Directory, LexisNexis Corporate Affiliations,* or in Business and Company Resource Center.

3. Apple Computer is Apple, Inc. It is easy to find the information on the first two items. Business and Company Resource Center, Hoover's Premium, *Standard & Poor's Register*, and the *Million Dollar Directory* all provide this information, though, in the case of *Standard & Poor's Register* and the *Million Dollar Directory,* it is necessary to consult the abbreviations tables, since both sources use different abbreviations for NASDAQ. *LexisNexis Corporate Affiliations* lists the ticker symbol, the stock exchange, and the transfer agent.

4. Business and Company Resource Center's company profile for Old Navy lists Gap, Inc. as the parent company. Hoover's Premium also lists Old Navy as a division of Gap, Inc. *LexisNexis Corporate Affiliation's* Master Index refers to The Gap, Inc., a public U.S. company. Under the listing for The Gap, Inc., one reads that Old Navy is a division of Gap, Inc. and has its own executives. The *Million Dollar Directory* has an entry for Old Navy, listing it as a subsidiary of Gap, Inc. but there is no further information about Old Navy under the listing for Gap, Inc. *Standard & Poor's Register* has any listing for Old Navy in Volume One or in the Cross Reference Index.

5. Although it is an enormous entity with many well-known products, Mars, Inc. is a private company and is not legally required to divulge financial information. Hoover's Premium (whose overview of Mars describes the company as "highly secretive") lists the 2006 sales as $21,000,000,000. *LexisNexis Corporate Affiliations* also lists financials but for the fiscal year 2005. Both the *Million Dollar Directory* and *Standard & Poor's Register* list revenue (the figures vary), but with no year provided. Business and Company and Resource Center also has an estimate for annual sales. It may be possible to gather more financial information from

the articles provided under Business and Company Resource Center's news and magazine tab. But the best sales figure that any source can provide is an estimate.

6. The *Million Dollar Directory, LexisNexis Corporate Affiliations,* and Hoover's Premium clearly list who comprises Halliburton's board of directors. Business and Company Resource Center does not give a discrete listing for board members, but officers' names have titles such as "Chairman of the Board" and "Director," making it easy to generate a list. *Standard & Poor's Register* provides this information also, but it can be tricky to locate. Part of the information is contained under "Other Directors;" however, when looking up individuals in *Standard & Poor's Register,* it is important to note any asterisk next to name. The "Key to Abbreviations" states that an asterisk denotes a member of the Board of Directors. In this case, it is crucial to look at all executive names in addition to those under "Other Directors."

7. Given the modest size of its sales and number of employees, this company is not included in the *Million Dollar Directory* or in *LexisNexis Corporate Affiliations*. Hoover's Premium has a brief entry, listing only one officer. *Standard & Poor's Register* and Business and Company Resource Center have the most information, providing names for the president, vice president, and treasurer.

8. *LexisNexis Corporate Affiliations* is the only source that provides information on a company's joint ventures.

6. CONSUMER MEDICAL AND HEALTH INFORMATION

OBJECTIVES

1. Using any resources available, identify the library's print resources on medical and drug information.
2. Be familiar with the Web sites for MedlinePlus and *The Merck Manual*.
3. Using any resources available, correctly answer 90 percent of all questions about medicine, health and medications.

TRAINING HANDOUT

Questions about health, illness, and medications are common in libraries. With the availability of high-quality information in print and on the Internet and the decline in time available for health professionals to spend providing health education and patient information during office visits, people turn to the library to help them find health information. When providing reference assistance to patrons with health-related inquiries, the paraprofessional should never attempt to provide medical advice or a diagnosis but should instead point the patron to the appropriate source of information and be ready to make a referral or alert a professional that follow-up may be required. The paraprofessional should also be sensitive to the fact that patrons may not be forthcoming about what they really need or may not be willing to provide specifics. The library provides access to numerous resources, both print and electronic, that can assist patrons in understanding health concerns.

Dorland's Illustrated Medical Dictionary **and** Stedman's Illustrated Medical Dictionary

Both of these dictionaries are standards in a medical reference collection. *Dorland's* (Saunders; online version available: www.dorlands.com) is considered by many to be "the dean of medical dictionaries"; however, *Stedman's* (Lippincott Williams & Wilkins; online version available: www.stedmans.com) is also accepted by many to be its peer. The two dictionaries are similar in authority, size, and comprehensiveness. However, due to editorial decisions, the two dictionaries will not always include the same definitions.

Physician's Desk Reference

This source (Montvale, NJ; Thomson PDR. Annual) is a handbook for physicians but it is a mainstay of any medical reference collection. Many patrons ask for it by name or by its acronym, the *PDR*. In cooperation with participating pharmaceutical manufacturers, The *Physician's Desk Reference* compiles the product information on the packages found in all available prescription drugs. Useful information includes dosage, composition, contraindications, warnings, use, and adverse effects. Some over-the-counter (OTC) and dietary supplements are also included. It is important to realize that the materials in the *Physician's Desk Reference* have been prepared by the manufacturer; the publisher only compiles and organizes the information. Three indices preface the "Product Information Section," which is arranged alphabetically by manufacturer. Those indices are "Manufacturers Index," "Brand and Generic Name Index," and "Product Category Index." The Brand and Generic Name Index should be used when the patron has the name of the drug or medication only. This index will refer to a page within the "Product Information" section. Also available is a "Product Identification Guide," which has color, life-sized photographs of the tablets and capsules.

The Merck Manual of Medical Information

The Merck Manual of Medical Information (available in print and online: www.merck.com/mmhe/index.html) is a condensed version of *The Merck Manual of Diagnosis and Therapy,* a tool for physicians, and is geared to the layperson. It is available in print, and as a public service, is provided on the Internet by Merck & Co., Inc., the pharmaceutical company. In the online version, the sections are listed alphabetically and are hyperlinked. There is also a hyperlinked index. A search box is available. This resource is a good place to begin for questions about diseases and medical conditions.

MedlinePlus

MedlinePlus (www.medlineplus.gov) is a service of the U.S. National Library of Medicine and the National Institutes of Health. This site includes links to health topics, information on drugs and supplements, a medical encyclopedia and dictionary, directories of doctors, dentists, hospitals, and more. A search engine is also available. Because it is a U.S. government site, it provides high-quality information that is free of charge. Some information is available in Spanish.

COMPARISON EXERCISES

Using both dictionaries, compare some definitions, illustrations, and the tables on arteries, muscles, and nerves.

Choose a medication and compare what information *Physicians Desk Reference* and the Drugs, Supplements, and Herbal Information portion of MedlinePlus each provide.

Search the same topic in MedlinePlus and the Web version of *The Merck Manual of Medical Information.*

PRACTICE QUESTIONS

1. What chemicals are in aspirin?
2. What is a Bozeman's speculum?
3. I have been prescribed Zyvox and want to know more about it.
4. What is the difference between Type 1 and Type 2 diabetes?
5. What are the chief functions of vitamin B_{12}?
6. What is the medical term for fear of germs?
7. I need a definition of raloxifene.
8. I need information on scores of the Glasgow Coma Scale.
9. What are some products used for Alzheimer's disease?
10. I need information on Crohn's disease.

Answers to Practice Questions

1. Both *Dorland's* and *Stedman's* have entries on aspirin (*Dorland's* is lengthier) but no information on the chemical makeup. The *Physician's Desk Reference,* however, has the most information about the chemical composition of aspirin, providing not only the formula, but the molecular weight, a diagram of the molecular structure, and a percentage breakdown. Aspirin is 60 percent carbon, 4.49 percent hydrogen, and 35.42 percent oxygen. Use the "Brand and Generic Name Index" to find aspirin under Bayer.
2. Both medical dictionaries have definitions of a speculum (plural is specula). *Stedman's* lists and defines

many different types of specula, including bivalve, duck-bill, Pedersen, but not Bozeman's. *Dorland's* has a definition of Bozeman's speculum.

3. The *Physician's Desk Reference* is a clear choice to answer this question. Looking at the "Brand and Generic Name Index" there are three entries for zyvox: zyvox injection, Zyvox for oral suspension, and Zyvox tablets, but all three entries are covered under the write-up in the Pharmacia and Upjohn section, which is more than five pages. Information more oriented to the layperson can be found in the "Drugs and Supplements" section of medlineplus.gov, which is from the American Society of Health-System Pharmacists (ASHP). The entry for Zyvox, the brand name, points to linezolid.

4. It is easy to find this information in *The Merck Manual of Medical Information,* which provides readable distinctions between Type 1 and Type 2 diabetes under "Types." Using the search term "diabetes types" yields several good results to choose from in MedlinePlus. *Dorland's* and *Stedman's* both provide brief information on the topic.

5. When choosing between the two dictionaries, *Dorland's* is a better choice to answer this question, clearly stating the vitamin is "necessary for the growth and replication of all body cells and the functioning of the nervous system." The entry in *Stedman's* might be more difficult for the layperson to understand. The "Drugs and Supplements" portion of MedlinePlus also provides good information; *Merck Manual* also provides a table with information on vitamins, including a column "Main Functions."

6. The appendix in *Dorland's* lists phobias in alphabetical order by "fear of." Fear of germs is microphobia. It is possible to look up "microphobia" in both dictionaries, but *Dorland's* is the source to consult if the term is not known.

7. Both *Stedman's* and *Dorland's* have entries for Raloxifene. However, *Stedman's* definition is lengthier because it is a "high-profile term;" *Stedman's* high-profile terms are concepts that "profoundly affect the practice of medicine and warrant more than the standard dictionary definition." Patrons wanting more than a definition can type the term into MedlinePlus' search

box and get a list of health topics (breast cancer, osteoporosis, etc.) as well as an entry under "Drugs and Supplements."

8. Both *Stedman's* and *Dorland's* have entries for "Glasgow Coma Scale" (the entry is under "scale") but *Stedman's* provides a table with monitored performance (e.g., verbal performance), reaction (e.g., coherent, no verbal reaction, etc.) and score (5 and 1, respectively). It is possible to answer the question searching MedlinePlus, but one must take the time to evaluate the results. *The Merck Manual* does not have any information.

9. The *Physician's Desk Reference* has a "Product Category Index," which classes products by category of prescription. There is a listing for "Alzheimer's Disease Management," along with the product name and the page number(s) for further information.

10. *The Merck Manual* has several pages devoted to Crohn's disease. A separate search in MedlinePlus provides numerous entries under "Health Topics," not to mention an entry in the Medical Encyclopedia, along with images.

RESOURCES

GENERAL ENCYCLOPEDIAS

Badke, William. 2008. "What to Do With Wikipedia." *Online* 32, no. 2 (March): 48–50. Badke discusses the popularity of Wikipedia and how "information professionals" should respond.

Berinstein, Paula. 2006. "Wikipedia and Britannica." *Searcher* 14, no. 3 (March): 16–26. Berinstein examines both Wikpedia and *Encyclopaedia Britannica,* including the contributors, audience, mission, and scope of each resource.

Cassell, Kay Ann, and Uma Hiremath. 2004. "Answering Questions About Anything and Everything—Encyclopedias." In *Reference and Information Services in the 21st Century: An Introduction,* 69–92. New York: Neal-Schuman Publishers. Provides overviews of encyclopedias, both print and electronic.

Crawford, Holly. 2001. "Encyclopedias." In *Reference and Information Services.* 3rd ed., edited by Richard E. Bopp and Linda C. Smith, 433–459. Englewood, CO: Libraries Unlimited. Describes uses and characteristics of the encyclopedias used in this module, along with other encyclopedias.

Katz, William A. 2002. "Encyclopedias: General and Subject Sets." In *Introduction to Reference Work: Volume One: Basic Information Services.* 8th ed., 213–276. NY: McGraw-Hill. In the chapter, Katz's textbook discusses the strengths and weaknesses of various encyclopedias.

Tenopir, Carol. 2007. "Quality Still Matters." *Library Journal* 132, no. 8 (May 1): 26. Carol Tenopir discusses the quality of entries in Wikipedia.

INTERNATIONAL INFORMATION

Cassell, Kay Ann, and Uma Hiremath. 2004. "Answering Questions That Require Handy Facts—Ready Reference Sources." In *Reference and Information Services in the 21st Century: An Introduction,* 93–110. New York: Neal-Schuman Publishers. This chapter provides overviews of *The Statesman's Yearbook*, *The CIA World Factbook,* and other ready reference sources.

Katz, William A. 2002. "Ready-Reference Sources." In *Introduction to Reference Work: Volume One: Basic Information Services.* 8th ed. NY: McGraw Hill. The section "Representative Yearbooks" discusses the strengths of *The Europa World Year Book, The Statesman's Yearbook,* as well as other resources for international information.

Miller, Susan. 2001. "Directories." In *Reference and Information Services,* 3rd ed., edited by Richard E. Bopp and Linda C. Smith, 331–356. Englewood, CO: Libraries Unlimited. Provides comparisons among *The Europa World Year Book, The Statesman's Yearbook,* and *The CIA World Factbook.*

STATISTICS

Katz, William A. 2002. "Ready-Reference Sources." In *Introduction to Reference Work: Volume One: Basic Information Services.* 8th ed. NY: McGraw-Hill. This chapter has a subsection "Statistics."
Mallory, Mary and Eric Forte. 2001. "Government Documents and Statistics Sources." In *Reference and Information Services,* 3rd ed., edited by Richard E. Bopp and Linda C. Smith, 537–593. Englewood, CO: Libraries Unlimited. Especially useful is the section "Statistical Sources."

GOVERNMENT INDIVIDUALS AND AGENCIES

Cassell, Kay Ann, and Uma Hiremath. 2004. "Answering Questions About Governments—Government Information Sources." In *Reference and Information Services in the 21st Century: An Introduction,* 213–230. New York: Neal-Schuman Publishers. Discusses the resources that can be used to answer the government information questions.
Mallory, Mary, and Eric Forte. 2001. "Government Documents and Statistics Sources." In *Reference and Information Services.* 3rd ed., edited by Richard E. Bopp and Linda C. Smith, 537–593. Englewood, CO: Libraries Unlimited. The section "General Facts and Directories" describes ready reference sources that can be used to answer questions about governments.

COMPANY INFORMATION

American Library Association. Reference and User Services Association. Business Reference and Services Section Education Committee. "Company and Industry Research" portion of "Core Competencies for Business Reference" Web site. Available: www.ala.org/ala/rusa/rusaourassoc/rusasections/brass/brassprotools/corecompetencies/corecompetenciescompany.cfm. Accessed: January 20, 2008. The Business Reference and Services Section (BRASS) maintains a Web page, "Core Competencies for Business Reference." These are basic subject guides for answering business reference questions in a general

reference setting. These guides present the information in a
"Frequently Asked Questions" format and provide important
definitions and information on key resources. The BRASS portion of
the American Library Association's Web site is a good starting point
for matters pertaining to business reference.

Cassell, Kay Ann, and Uma Hiremath. 2004. "Answering Questions
About Health, Law, and Business—Special Guidelines and Sources."
In *Reference and Information Services in the 21st Century: An
Introduction,* 155–182. New York: Neal-Schuman Publishers. In
addition to discussing resources, this chapter also points out that
medical, legal and business questions are especially sensitive and
specialized.

Tucker, James Gory. 2004. "Getting Down to Business: Library Staff
Training." *Reference Services Review* 32, no. 3: 293–301. Tucker
presents a model program to train staff for business reference.

CONSUMER MEDICAL AND HEALTH INFORMATION

Boorkman, Jo Anne, Jeffrey T. Huber, and Fred W. Roper. 2004.
Introduction to Reference Sources in the Health Sciences. 4th ed.
Neal-Schuman Publishers. Presents in-depth information about
sources in the health sciences. One chapter is devoted to consumer
health sources.

Cassell, Kay Ann, and Uma Hiremath. 2004. "Answering Questions
About Health, Law, and Business—Special Guidelines and Sources."
In *Reference and Information Services in the 21st Century: An
Introduction,* 155–182. New York: Neal-Schuman Publishers. In
addition to discussing resources, this chapter also points out that
medical, legal, and business questions are especially sensitive and
specialized.

Gillaspy, Mary L. 2005. "Factors Affecting the Provision of Consumer
Health Information in Public Libraries: The Last Five Years." *Library
Trends* 53, no. 3: 480–495. Gillaspy discusses several changes
impacting libraries that provide consumer health information to the
public, including the amount of consumer health information
available, the Internet, and health professionals' lack of time to
discuss health issues with patients.

8 COMMUNICATION SKILLS

To successfully answer questions at the reference desk and/or make referrals, it is important that paraprofessionals be able to communicate effectively with patrons. Even if the paraprofessional is only responsible for answering ready reference, directional or other routine questions, it is necessary to train him or her how to communicate at the reference desk. Many users do not or cannot ask exactly what they are looking for at first, and the question cannot be accepted at face value. Even if the paraprofessional does not end up answering the question, she or he should still be trained in the communication skills that will give the patron a chance to elaborate on what is needed. Staff not trained in these skills may attempt to answer all questions, referring only those they feel they cannot answer (Emmick, 1985). The staff member will provide resources that are truly helpful or will make a proper referral (Ross, 2003). This chapter outlines specific communication issues, presents several nonverbal and verbal skills necessary for a successful communication, handling categories of questions, addresses the necessity of the reference interview, defines the reference interview, presents special reference interview situations, and suggests how to train for reference interview behaviors and skills.

HOW USERS ASK QUESTIONS

It is helpful for the paraprofessional to have a general idea of how people think about information and ask questions at the library. This is the first step in getting the patron the information and resources he or she needs. By having this understanding, the employee will better understand the need for, and importance of, good communication skills and proper referrals. The supervisor must make the employee aware that patrons often do not ask for what they really want. Many patron requests appear simple and easy to answer but are not; the initial question does not resemble the patron's true information need. Some examples are:

Question asked: Can you tell me where your books on airplanes are?

Information need: Patron wants information on overcoming fear of flying.

Question asked: You have one-volume biographical directories, don't you?

Information need: Patron wants to know where Booker T. Washington is buried.

Question asked: Do you have cookbooks with soufflé recipes?

Information need: Patron wants to know what makes soufflés rise.

(Ross, Nilsen, and Dewdney, 2002)

In many cases, where the patron's initial question differs from the real question, there are certain patterns and repeated problems. The supervisor can point out these pitfalls (along with examples) to the staff member so that he or she is aware of them. Some examples are:

1. Users ask for something very broad and general when they really want something very specific. The patron may ask, "Where is your Japanese History section?" when the need is much more precise—a school assignment to find biographical material on a particular Japanese emperor.

2. Users ask for something specific but there is a mismatch between what they request and what will help them. The user might ask about a specific database simply because a friend had used it successfully for a literature paper, when another database or other resource would be better for a history paper.

3. Users have a limited understanding how the library system works and may ask their initial question in a way that they think meets the system's requirements. This understanding can be oversimplified, incomplete, or wrong (Ross, Nilsen, and Dewdney, 2002). For example, a patron might state the following interchangeably to get a book from Branch X to Branch Y:

   A. I would like to put a book on hold.
   B. I would like to put a book on reserve.
   C. I would like to get a book through interlibrary loan.
   D. I would like you to hold a book for me.

In the library system, these are four discrete things:

Phrase A is the library term for the service the patron actually wants.

Phrase B is the library service to put a book aside for a long time where no one can check it out.

Phrase C gets a book from an out-of-town library.

Phrase D: the librarian goes to the shelf and gets the book for the patron and sets it aside to for the patron to pick up later.

Similarly, a patron may ask, "Do you have books on . . ." because he or she thinks that all information is contained in books.

4. The keywords in patrons' questions are vague. Causes of this can be patron pronunciation or how the staff member heard something. Examples include a telephone request in which the librarian heard the request for information on "Stalin" and retrieved titles of books on Russian History. "1 was interested in hair!" The patron had actually asked for information about "styling." A word that has different meanings can also cause confusion: "Do you have information on remedial plants?" Does the word plant refer to a living thing or a facility such as a factory?

5. The user's question is a reconstruction. The user tries to remember terms or details but gets it wrong. Example: Patron asks for a book, *The Red Shoe,* but wants *Balzac and the Little Chinese Seamstress.* The reconstruction was based on the book cover, featuring a red shoe.

Understanding that these communication problems exist will help the paraprofessional interact more effectively with patrons at the reference desk (Ross, Nilsen, and Dewdney, 2002).

SETTING THE STAGE

APPROACHABILITY

In order for a reference transaction to take place, the staff member should appear approachable, signaling that he or she is available and willing to help (Ross, Nilsen, and Dewdney, 2002). Behaviors a person can exhibit to encourage questions from library patrons include:

- smiling,
- greeting,
- establishing eye contact with the user,
- asking a user if he or she needs assistance, and
- remaining visible (Bopp, 2001).

The supervisor should communicate to the paraprofessional that, while at the reference desk, service to patrons is the first priority, and he or she should stop all other activities when patrons approach and focus on the patron. This is important if the employee is given other duties to perform while at the desk, such as filing or magazine check-in. The supervisor should encourage the staff member to look up frequently and avoid becoming absorbed in work, in conversations with coworkers, or with what is on the computer screen. If the desk is busy, the paraprofessional should make every effort to acknowledge those patrons waiting for service (RUSA, 2004).

INTEREST

Closely related to approachability is interest. Not every reference transaction will be stimulating or exciting, especially if the paraprofessional is responsible for routine and repetitive questions. Nevertheless, the question is important to the patron, and the employee should acknowledge this. The staff member must be engaged in the patron's informational need and demonstrate commitment to providing assistance. If the paraprofessional fails to show interest, the patron, after asking the initial question, may be hesitant to further discuss what he or she is looking for. Suggested behavior includes:

- Face the patron when speaking and listening.
- Maintain eye contact with the patron.
- Confirm understanding of the question by positive body language, such as nodding, smiling, or by a verbal acknowledgment.
- Try to be at eye level with the patron.
- Avoid "closed" postures, such as crossing your arms. (RUSA, 2004; Ross, Nilsen, and Dewdney, 2002)

These behaviors must not be abandoned after the reference transaction begins but should be maintained throughout the entire exchange. The goal is to let the patron know that the library is a welcoming place and that employees wish to assist with any information need.

COMMUNICATION SKILLS FOR ROUTINE QUESTIONS

When preparing to train the paraprofessional about communication skills, the supervisor should think about the types of questions that are asked. Not all routine questions are alike. Some are straightforward and may require a simple answer; these tend to be directional questions. Other requests may require that the paraprofessional provide some sort of assistance. Still others will require professional expertise and a referral. Some requests that appear routine may require some questioning skills. The supervisor should, as much as possible, try to categorize the questions and provide the paraprofessional guidelines on how to respond.

Examples of clear-cut questions include:

- What are your hours?
- Where is the bathroom, water fountain, etc.?
- Do you have a drink machine?
- Where do I get . . . [e.g., ILL requests, print reserves]?
- Where is building X?
- Do you have . . . [e.g., a class schedule, campus catalog, campus directory]?

The paraprofessional can respond to the question as asked.

Examples of questions that do not require professional expertise, but that do require patron assistance might be necessary:

- Where do you print?
- Where is the scanner?
- Where is the photocopier?
- Where do I go to check out a book?
- What floor are these books on?

Suggested responses to the above questions: The paraprofessional should provide directions and ask if assistance is needed or offer to help.

The employee should also be aware of how to respond when questions are vague. The following questions involve equipment or processes:

- Where I can print copies? (Does the patron mean printing from a computer or making photocopies?)
- How can I get reserves? (Is the patron referring to print or electronic reserves?)

- How do I search for a book if I have the call number? (Is the patron asking about searching catalogs or finding a book on the shelf?)

If it is not clear to the paraprofessional what the patron wants, the supervisor should emphasize that it is acceptable to ask for some clarification. This practice is preferable to sending the patron to the wrong place or getting the wrong material.

There are questions and or phrases that will provide a cue to the paraprofessional that he or she should immediately make a referral to a professional librarian. Examples:

- I am doing a paper on X? Where do I start?
- I can't find anything on my topic. I've searched everywhere.
- I have an assignment on . . .
- I've never been to the library before but my professor told me . . .

Suggested response: Let me call a librarian for you. He/she will be able to provide the fastest and most complete assistance.

Perhaps the trickiest questions are those that appear simple but might not be. Examples include:

- Where are the reference books?
- Where are the magazines?
- Do you have . . . [name of specific book, reference work, database]?

The patron may really need the specific book, in which case the paraprofessional can probably handle the question; or, there may be an assignment, and the patron should be referred to a professional librarian.

In cases like these, it is helpful for the supervisor to compile a list of questions to be aware of that require some questioning skills; the paraprofessional should respond to the patron's question as asked but then might follow up with a question designed to get the patron to open up more. For example:

- "The reference books are in the room to our left. It's quite a big area. If you could tell me more about what you are looking for, I'd be able to provide you with more specific directions."
- "Yes, we have that database. We also have other resources that may be helpful. Was there something specific you were looking for?"

If the patron responds that this is for an assignment, this is the time for a referral. If the patron insists on using the specific resources he or she initially requested, a good habit could be for the paraprofessional to alert the professional librarian, who could then rove and ask whether the patron is finding everything he or she needs. If no professional librarian is on duty, the paraprofessional should follow up and, if needed, make referrals.

Not all queries can be neatly categorized, and there will be some instances where certain questions fall through the cracks. The supervisor should take the time to discuss these exceptions with the paraprofessional. Coaching or feedback sessions (discussed in Chapter 9, "Performance Management") are excellent opportunities to do this. Even if the staff member is answering a core list of "safe" questions, the supervisor should meet with him or her to discuss how he or she responded to the questions, how a referral was made, and whether a referral was needed (Emmick, 1985).

It is important for the paraprofessional to end all transactions smoothly, however brief or routine. Good closure should let the patron know the transaction is completed with the option to return if more help or information is needed. To wrap up the transaction smoothly, it is recommended to use verbal skills rather than nonverbal skills, such as moving away, change in eye contact, or initiating a transaction with another patron. Verbal cues can include a phrase such as, "Please come back if you need any more help." The paraprofessional can ask the user if the question was completely answered and encourage him or her to return with another information need. The patron can answer yes; or, he or she has another chance to expand on what he or she wanted.

MAKING REFERRALS

It is important that, if the paraprofessional makes a referral, it be done smoothly; patrons should never be left to pursue matters on their own (Flanagan and Horowitz, 2000). The paraprofessional should never refer the patron to another person, floor, or agency without providing helpful information. If paraprofessionals will be making referrals, it is important that they know how to do so in a way that does not convey to the patron that the staff member is simply trying to "get rid of them." The supervisor should communicate to the staff member that, if he or she feels she is unable to answer the question, or according to the guidelines established during the planning stages (Chapter 2), certain steps must take place for a proper referral. If the paraprofessional is referring the patron to another department, the supervisor should stress the importance of explaining to the patron why he or she is being directed elsewhere or calling first to ensure that someone is there to help them (Bopp, 2001). When referring the patron to another

```
┌─────────────────────────────────────────────────────────┐
│  Patron Needs:                                            │
│                                                           │
│  Title:            _____   │
│                                                           │
│  Call Number:      _____   │
│                                                           │
│                                                           │
│  Subject:          _____   │
│                                                           │
│  Location:         _____   │
│                                                           │
│  Circulating                                              │
│  Reference                                                │
│  Periodicals                                              │
│                                                           │
│                                                           │
│  Staff Member:  _____    │
│                                                           │
│  Date:             _____   │
├─────────────────────────────────────────────────────────┤
│  Figure 8.1.  Reference Referral                          │
└─────────────────────────────────────────────────────────┘
```

staff member in another location, the staff member should call ahead and explain as much as possible so that the patron does not need to start from scratch. He or she should facilitate this referral by writing down as much information as possible, such as information consulted, sources already checked, and the source(s) needed (RUSQ, 2004). A referral slip, such as those in Figures 8.1 and 8.2, can be useful. If the employee is not working alone but feels she or he must get another person to answer the question, this must be done in a manner that is positive and patron oriented. For example:

- "Please let me get XXXX; she would be able to provide you with the most complete information."
- "I don't know, but I'll get someone to help you."

In instances when the staff member must work alone, the supervisor should ensure that mechanisms are in place for the paraprofessional to get the appropriate information to the right person. This might be an action such as encouraging the patron to use an e-mail reference service if one is available or the use of a referral slip, such as those in Figures 8.1 and 8.2. In these cases, the employee should make it clear to the patron when a librarian or staff member will be getting back to him or her.

Date: _____

Patron Name: _____

Telephone: _____

Best time to be reached:

Day _____   Night _____

E-mail: _____

Request/Subject (Please be a specific as possible):

_____

_____

_____

_____

Important terms, words, concepts:

_____

_____

_____

_____

Preferred format (circle as many as necessary):

Journal articles   Books   Newspapers

Web sites   Other _____

Date needed by: _____

Thank you. A Librarian will contact you within 24 hours (48 hours for weekends).

Figure 8.2. Referral Form

THE REFERENCE INTERVIEW

"The reference interview is the heart of the reference transaction and is crucial to the success of the process. The [service provider] must be effective in identifying the patron's information needs and must do so in a manner that keeps patrons at ease. Strong listening and questioning skills are necessary for a positive interaction" (RUSA, 2004, p. 16).

A library may be fortunate enough to have talented paraprofessionals who show an aptitude for reference work or have the opportunity to utilize MLS students. In cases like this, the library may wish to train the paraprofessional to answer more complex questions and conduct a reference interview.

WHAT IS A REFERENCE INTERVIEW?

The reference interview is "a conversation **between** a reference staff member and a user, the goal of which is to ascertain the user's information need" (Bopp, 2001, p. 47; emphasis added). The prefix "inter" means between or among. The reference interview is neither as formal as the word "interview" would indicate, nor as informal as a conversation. However, interviews are conversations with a purpose, and the same can be said of a reference interview. The library employee must focus on the user and strive to understand the patron's need (Bopp, 2001). A reference interview is a two-way process involving both the patron and staff member. The patron knows why he or she needs the information, and the service provider understands the library and the information. By working together, ideally, the staff member will connect the patron with the resource(s) needed (Ross, 2003). Some of the information that must be gathered during the reference interview includes:

1. What kind of information is needed? If the question is about Edgar Allan Poe, does the patron need quick factual information about Poe? Biographical information? Criticism and interpretations about Poe's works?
2. How much information is needed and what information does the patron already have?
3. How is the information going to be used? Is it to settle a bet? For a research paper? For the homework assignment of someone's child?
4. How much does the user already know about the subject? Will an introductory encyclopedia suffice or are more advanced materials needed?
5. How much time does the patron wish to spend finding and using the information?
6. When is the information needed? Is there a deadline? (Katz, 2002)

Librarians have taken many approaches to the reference interview. Figure 8.3 summarizes a few of these.

Different people have various steps to the reference interview. Examples follow.

1. Open the interview
2. Negotiate the question
3. Search for the information
4. Communicate the information to the user
5. Close the interview

Source: From Bopp, Richard E. 2001. "The Reference Interview." In *Reference and Information Services,* 3rd ed., edited by Richard E. Bopp and Linda C. Smith, 47–68. Englewood, Colorado: Libraries Unlimited.

1. Approachability
2. Interest
3. Listening
4. Searching
5. Follow Up

Source: From Reference and User Services Association Division (RUSA). Reference Services Section. Management of Reference Committee. 2004. "Guidelines for Behavioral Performance of Reference and Information Service Providers." *Reference and User Services Quarterly* 44(Fall): 14–17.

1. Establish contact with the user
2. Find out user's need
3. Confirm that answer provided is what was needed.

Source: From Ross, Catherine Sheldrick, Kristi Nilsen, and Patricia Dewdney. *Conducting the Reference Interview: A How-To-Do-It Manual for Librarians* (p. 5). New York: Neal-Schuman Publishers, 2002.

1. Informal Interaction (build a rapport)
2. Questioning (define and negotiate the request)
3. Locate the information/search for the answer
4. Communicate the response/Close the interview

Source: From Sutton, Ellen D., and Leslie Edmonds Holt. 1995. "The Reference Interview." In *Reference and Information Services: An Introduction,* edited by Richard E. Bopp and Linda C. Smith, 42–58. Englewood, CO: Libraries Unlimited.

Figure 8.3. In a Nutshell: Steps of the Reference Interview

NEGOTIATING THE QUESTION

As with answering routine questions, the behaviors of approachability and demonstrating interest should be present so that the patron will ask the question. Once the patron has asked the question, the staff member must determine the true nature of the request. Good listening and inquiring skills are crucial at this stage and contribute to the success of the reference interview (RUSA, 2004).

LISTENING SKILLS

Honed listening is the basis of oral communication. Weak listening or not listening at all can lead to a poor reference interview (Ross, Nilsen, and Dewdney, 2002). Effective listening involves the following:

1. Focus and pay close attention. It can be difficult to concentrate and listen when the phone is ringing and there is a buzz of activity around the reference desk. The supervisor should encourage the employee to avoid trying to save time by thinking about the search strategy during the listening phase. Resisting the urge to speed up the process can be difficult, especially if the desk is busy. However, a lapse in listening could cause the paraprofessional to miss important information, the result being the provision of incorrect or incomplete information. In this case, time is not gained but lost, and the service provided is poor. The staff member should never think about the strategy until the question is fully understood (Bopp, 2001).

2. Make it clear to the other person that he or she (paraprofessional) is listening. This is where the nonverbal behaviors such as establishing and maintaining eye contact, nodding, acknowledging, and using brief encouraging phrases such as "I see" or "go on" come into play.

3. Give the user time to answer questions.

4. Do not interrupt or try to complete the patron's sentence. Another predictable way for a reference interview to go wrong is for the service provider to interrupt at inappropriate times (Ross, Nilsen, and Dewdney, 2002).

INQUIRING SKILLS

How does one get from the question, "You have one-volume biographical directories, don't you?" to finding out that what the patron really wants to know is where Booker T. Washington is buried? The answer is asking the right questions. There are a variety of techniques to use when trying to find out what the patron really wants (Ross, Nilsen, and Dewdney, 2002).

Open and Closed Questions

Open questions encourage the patron to elaborate on what she or he needs. Think of these as allowing the user to "open up." Open questions are most

To find out what a person wants in order to supply the need:

- What sort of thing are you looking for?
- What information would you like on this?
- What sort of material do you have in mind?
- What requirements do you have for the project?

To get a description of a problem or event:

- What have you done about this question so far?
- Where did you hear about this?

To encourage the person to elaborate:

- What aspect of X concerns you?
- What else can you tell me about X?
- Perhaps if you tell me more about this problem/project, I could make some suggestions.

To get clarification:

- What do you mean by X?
- What would be an example of that? Can you give me an example? Please give me an example.
- Can you help me to understand X?

Figure 8.4. Some Useful Open Questions

helpful in the beginning stage of the reference interview when the staff member is trying to determine the type of information needed. Examples of open questions include "Can you tell me more about what you are looking for?" "I think I understand what you need. Can you provide me with more detail?" (Bopp, 2001). Open questions begin with Who, What, Why, Where, When, or How (e.g., What would you like to know about . . . ? How did you hear about . . . ? Where did you read about . . . ?). Use open questions to:

- hear the patron state in his or her own words the nature of a problem or situation;
- encourage the other person to talk; and
- avoid guessing or making assumptions. (Ross, Nilsen, and Dewdney, 2002)

Figure 8.4 has some examples of open questions that will encourage the patron to more fully explain his or her information need.

Closed questions, on the other hand, tend to elicit short responses, such as "yes" or "no." Examples are "Do you need scholarly or popular literature?" or "Have you checked the catalog?" In general, the middle or later part of the reference interview is the best time to ask closed questions; by that time, the topic should be understood and requirements such as format or time period need to be pinpointed (Bopp, 2001). A closed question can be used to focus a wandering conversation and to verify understanding of the topic (Ross, Nilsen, and Dewdney, 2002). If the paraprofessional drifts toward asking exclusively closed questions, there is the danger of the interview resembling an interrogation and derailing the interview process.

Paraphrase and Summarize

After negotiating the questions using the above skills, it is wise for the paraprofessional to reflect back to the user his or her understanding of the question. This practice will allow the patron to confirm that the employee has grasped what is needed or to provide correction if the case is otherwise. This reflection can be done in two ways: (1) paraphrasing, and (2) summarizing. Paraphrasing restates the essence of the question, and can be introduced by a clause such as:

- So you are looking for . . .
- You mean . . .
- What you need . . .

Summarizing is similar to paraphrasing but is lengthier. It can be a good conclusion to the interview prior to searching for resources (Ross, Nilsen, Dewdney, 2002).

INCLUSION

Once the staff member has clarified the question, it is time to move on to the search process and to locate the information for the patron. Whenever possible, the search process should be a joint effort, with the staff member accompanying the patron to the online catalog, the computer workstation, or the book stacks (Bopp, 2001). The paraprofessional should also include the patron in the search process. This practice, known as inclusion, is an effective way to prevent communication accidents, a method of reassuring the user that he or she is being helped, and a confirmation that the staff member is interested in providing assistance. A simple way to include the patron is to explain to him or her, what is being done, why it is being done, and what to expect. The user remains a partner in the process and the communication channel remains open because the staff member can continue to discuss the question during the search process until the information is located (Ross, Nilsen, and Dewdney, 2002).

CLOSURE AND FOLLOW-UP

As with routine questions, closing the reference interview properly is as important as beginning it, because this exchange will influence the final impression the patron will have of the library reference service; it will also impact how satisfied the patron is with the information provided (Bopp, 2001). When finishing up a reference interview, the paraprofessional should employ the same behaviors for closure and follow up as with routine questions. Because the reference interview entails a more complex query than routine questions, the use of follow-up questions is especially crucial. Follow-up questions allow the staff member to discover and recover from communication accidents while the patron is still in the library.

It is important for the paraprofessional to avoid sending a person off without a helpful answer (Ross, 2003). Follow-up is extremely important, especially if the reference desk is very busy. In the case of several people waiting for help, it may be in everyone's best interest to get the patrons started, prompting them to come back for more assistance with a statement such as: "If that is not what you are looking for, please come back." Roving is an excellent follow-up technique. Not all people will take advantage of the additional chances a follow-up question provides, especially if they perceive the staff member as being too busy with other patrons. Roving enables the staff member to seek out the patron and, if he or she appears to be having difficulties, offer assistance again. A well-conducted reference interview has occurred when the service provider has listened while encouraging the patron to talk and expand on the topic as much as possible and has employed various communication strategies to ensure that the patron was fully understood (Ross, Nilsen, and Dewdney, 2002).

TELEPHONE REFERENCE INTERVIEW

Not only do patrons ask for assistance in person, but they also ask for it over the telephone. The reference interview must still occur, albeit in a modified form. The telephone reference interview should incorporate many of the behaviors of the in-person interview: acknowledgement, minimal encouragers, clarification, verification, and of course, listening. What is missing are the visual cues. Even though these signals are absent, the service provider still conveys to the patron that he or she is approachable and interested, as well as creates an environment that encourages the patron to elaborate. This is achieved by using a friendly tone of voice. Sound can convey nonverbal cues, such as enthusiasm, interest, irritation, or uncertainty. In addition, because the user is not physically present to participate, the service provider must fully understand what is needed. It is helpful to write down as much information as possible and to repeat the question to the patron to verify understanding (Bopp, 2001; Ross, Nilsen, and Dewdney, 2002).

Inclusion is also important. The paraprofessional should make every effort to keep the patron apprised of what he or he is doing ("I'll need to check our business directories, which could take a few minutes. Do you mind holding?") and avoid putting the caller on hold for excessive periods of time.

If the question cannot be answered immediately, reference policy may allow for (or even dictate) a callback. If the paraprofessional exercises such an option, he or she must make it clear to the patron that he or she will be contacted later with the information and provided with a time frame in which to expect the callback. If the paraprofessional is setting aside materials for the patron to look at later, he or she should make it clear what the materials are, where they can be found, and if applicable, how long the materials will be set aside. The staff member should also communicate this to other staff members if he or she is not available when the patron comes in.

Closure, follow-up, and referral are also part of the telephone reference interview. If further assistance is required, the paraprofessional should encourage the patron to call back, send an e-mail, or visit the library. If the patron is being transferred to another department, the paraprofessional should explain to the patron why he or she is being transferred and that he or she will be put on hold while the paraprofessional alerts the other staff member. As with in-person referrals, the employee should provide the staff of other departments with as much information as possible about what the patron needs.

ELECTRONIC REFERENCE INTERVIEW

If the paraprofessional will be providing real-time virtual reference service (chat, instant messaging, etc.), he or she will need to be aware of the challenges of communicating with patrons in the online environment. The most important difference between communicating in the online environment, as opposed to in person or on the telephone, is that both visual and audio cues are lacking. There is no tone of voice, eye contact, body language, or facial expressions. The likelihood of miscommunication is increased. Some additional hallmarks of chat and IM communication are:

- Importance of typing, writing, and spelling skills
- Fast pace (and possible impatience)
- Reduced inhibitions
- Use of emoticons and abbreviations (e.g., BRB for Be Right Back, K for OK)

When communicating online, the paraprofessional should use short but informative and frequent messages. The time to compose a long message can be misinterpreted as ignoring the patron. The employee should always keep the patron apprised of what he or she is doing:

- "I am checking the online catalog."
- "I want to check one more resource."
- "Still checking . . ."
- "I am going to send you a link to a Web page."

The paraprofessional also should be aware of how to choose words when writing. Because there is no tone of voice, some things that are perfectly fine when spoken may not be the best choice when writing. Consider the difference between:

- "Did you check the database Business and Company Resource Center?" and
- "Could you please tell me if you've already checked the database Business and Company Resource Center?"

It is important to be concise without being impolite when communicating via online messages. For example, responding with a simple "yes" or "no" to a question online might be construed as rude when it is perfectly acceptable in person.

The supervisor should take some time to have the paraprofessional practice with the software along with communication skills. The paraprofessional may have to tailor the language used in the virtual reference interview, depending on the software features. The more basic the software (e.g., lack of ability to push pages or co-browse), the more the paraprofessional will have to communicate. Likewise, if the software has these options, the paraprofessional will have to learn to let the user know what is happening ("I am about to 'push' you a Web page with the information you need. Please tell me when you see it.").

In the virtual environment, there is no opportunity to give a nonverbal signal that the transaction is over. Once the answer is found, the paraprofessional should ask if there is anything else that is needed and encourage the patron to return if there are any other questions. If the patron does not respond, the paraprofessional should be trained to inform the patron that it has been a while since he or she has communicated and that the session is now ending, and encourage the patron to come back if there any questions.

Depending on the virtual reference software, the supervisor will have to instruct the paraprofessional on how to refer a difficult question. If a professional librarian is logged onto virtual reference at the same time and the software permits it, the paraprofessional may be able to employ language similar to that used in person and on the telephone to electronically "transfer" the patron. However, if the paraprofessional is working alone or the software does not permit, the paraprofessional may have to ask the patron to submit the question via e-mail or pay a visit to the library to speak to a professional librarian, or contact a subject or research specialist (Ronan, 2003).

It is important for the paraprofessional to remember that, while taking place online, many of the same qualities of in-person reference still apply to virtual reference. The paraprofessional must be able to search, include the patron, evaluate Internet sources for reliability, make a proper referral, and communicate well (Meola and Stormont, 2002). Before having the paraprofessional provide virtual reference, the supervisor should ensure that the paraprofessional is well grounded in basic reference sources, navigating the library Web page, using the online catalog, possibly some core databases, using the virtual reference software, and online communication. The supervisor should review transcripts (and inform the paraprofessional that this will occur) and provide feedback and coaching to improve skills.

SPECIAL PATRONS

The supervisor must alert the paraprofessional to some of the challenges that exist when conducting a reference interview with certain groups of patrons. The same techniques, such as being approachable, putting the patron at ease, and involving the patron hold true. However, there are additional considerations of which the paraprofessional should be aware.

CHILDREN AND YOUNG ADULTS

The paraprofessional should treat questions from children and young adults as seriously as a question from an adult. The staff member must also take into consideration that children and young adults differ developmentally from adults. This group might have less experience with a library and information sources and may not know what to expect. Extra effort should be made to accompany a child or young adult to the shelves. Children and young adults may not have the refined communication skills of an adult; their vocabulary may be more limited, they may mispronounce words, and they may still be learning how to frame questions. The reference interview may take a bit longer and patience is required.

Also, children and teens may be hesitant to ask for help; it is better to approach them and ask whether they are finding what they need rather than if they need help. Students may not know library terminology. Avoid use of library jargon, even terms that do not seem like jargon such as "fiction" and "nonfiction." If library terminology must be used, then it should be explained ("Nonfiction is a book with facts") (Riedling, 2000; Ross, Nilsen, and Dewdney, 2002).

PATRONS WITH DISABILITIES

"Libraries must not discriminate against individuals with disabilities and shall ensure that individuals with disabilities have equal access to library resources" (ALA, 2001). Disabilities can include speech disorders, hearing impediments, visual impairments, and limited mobility. Library staff members should expect to respond to the information needs of persons with disabilities and must possess the appropriate communication to assist this group.

When assisting a hearing-impaired person, it is important to always face the person directly in order to facilitate lip reading and, if needed, to allow the patron to turn a better ear toward the service provider. Facing the patron will also allow the other person to see facial expressions. Because the ability to see expressions is important in these cases, movements that would impair lip reading or cause confusion should be avoided. Speaking louder usually will not help the situation; it may have the opposite effect and embarrass the person. The service provider should use a normal tone of voice, enunciating without exaggeration. Finally, writing a message can be effective in getting a message across if other communication does not work. If the visually impaired patron has a reader or someone to assist him or her speak to the patron, not the other person. When providing directions, it is important to be explicit as possible, avoiding terms such as "this way," "that way," or "over there." If a patron is in a wheelchair, it is effective for the service provider to sit down so that he or she is at eye level; this also helps to put the patron at ease and allows the staff member and the patron to see each other's facial expressions and hear each other more clearly (Jennerich and Jennerich, 1997).

> **Working with Disabled Patrons**
>
> - Focus on the person, not the disability.
> - Speak directly to the patron, not to a companion.
> - Express empathy, not pity or sympathy.
> - Use written communication if needed. (Jennerich and Jennerich, 1997, pp. 81–83)

TEACHING COMMUNICATION SKILLS

It is up to individual libraries to determine how many of these communication skills the paraprofessional will be required to exhibit. There are several ways to teach paraprofessionals the skills necessary for a reference interview. A good way to impart the importance of these behaviors to the paraprofessional is for the supervisor, the professional librarians, and other staff to "model" the desired behavior. Employees are more likely to demonstrate a behavior if they see it in others. Expecting the staff member to look approachable and show interest when professionals do not do so is counterproductive. The paraprofessional will receive mixed messages and may think, "If they don't do it, why should I?"

VIDEOS, ARTICLES, AND BOOKS

Numerous print materials focus on the reference interview. It can be helpful to have the staff member read about the process so that he or she is aware of what the issues are. Even reading about the difference between open and closed questions will make the staff member more conscious of communication at the reference desk. *Conducting the Reference Interview: A How-To-Do-It Manual for Librarians,* by Ross, Nilsen, and Dewdney (2002), is an excellent resource. This very readable and practical book goes in depth with communication issues and question-asking skills and provides a wealth of hints and exercises for practice.

There are also videos. Videos tend to cover the same materials as the books and articles but provide the staff member with a chance to see demonstrations of what is being discussed. An additional advantage to a video is that it can be paused, discussed, and replayed.

WORKSHOPS

Workshops are an effective way to teach verbal and nonverbal skills. These can include materials from videos and readings, but it is best to have some kind of active learning, such as role-playing. If there is resistance to the role-playing, as noted in Chapter 2, then a demonstration of a reference interview with commentary by the trainer and critique of techniques by the staff member might also be effective (What worked? What did not work?). There may be staff development opportunities outside the library such as a workshop at a conference.

MICROTRAINING AND PRACTICE

One approach to teach reference interview skills to a paraprofessional is microtraining. This method starts with mastering the basics, such as eye contact, welcoming body language, and acknowledgment. These skills are learned first because, executed well, they create a climate that facilitates communication between the service provider and the patron. In this training module, the paraprofessional would learn the verbal skills of acknowledgement, restatement, and minimal encouraging before moving on to more complex verbal skills such as open and closed questioning. The steps are:

1. Supervisor defines the skill(s) and identifies the function to the paraprofessional.
2. The staff member observes the supervisor and other staff members modeling the behavior.
3. The paraprofessional reads about the skill and the concepts behind it.

4. The paraprofessional practices the skill in a situation that provides feedback, such as a workshop.

5. The employee uses the skill in a real situation and sees what happens.

The paraprofessional should be taught and given the opportunity to master one skill at a time (Ross, Nilsen, and Dewdney, 2002).

Reading materials, videos, role-playing, and workshops are all helpful but they are no substitute for real life. The best way for the staff member to learn how to conduct the reference interview is to let him or her practice . . . and make mistakes. It is best to practice one skill at a time, such as acknowledgment. Let the paraprofessional learn from missed opportunities and communication accidents. The supervisor might want to ensure that he or she is scheduled to work with the paraprofessional at the desk from time to time. These times can be a learning opportunity. The supervisor can have the paraprofessional observe and then provide the paraprofessional with a breakdown of the reference interview components. The supervisor can point out his or her own mistakes and how it would be done differently the next time. The supervisor can also coach the staff member and provide feedback (Ross, Nilsen, and Dewdney, 2002). A more in-depth discussion of coaching and feedback can be found in Chapter 9, "Performance Management."

Being able to communicate well is essential to connecting patrons with the services they need. In addition, several traits have been identified as being crucial to a successful reference transaction; these qualities include being approachable and demonstrating interest. Patrons tend to be satisfied with a reference transaction based on their perceptions on how helpful the service provider was. In one analysis, patrons valued the librarian being "nice, helpful, and pleasant" (Durrance, 1989, 1995). A good service provider communicates and listens well, but he or she also imparts the impression that he or she wants to help at present and in the future (Ross, Nilsen, and Dewdney, 2002). Helpfulness is a behavior that can be used at any level of public service. It is important for paraprofessionals to be trained in communication skills, along with searching and using reference sources. Tools and sources may change, but the reference process will always begin with good communication (Tyckoson, 2003).

REFERENCES

American Library Association. 2001. Association of Specialized and Cooperative Library Agencies. "Library Services for People with Disabilities Policy." Available: www.ala.org/ala/ascla/asclaissues/

libraryservices.cfm. Accessed: September 22, 2008. Provides recommendations for library services for people with disabilities.

Bopp, Richard E. 2001. "The Reference Interview." In *Reference and Information Services,* 3rd ed., edited by Richard E. Bopp and Linda C. Smith, 47–68. Englewood, CO: Libraries Unlimited. A textbook approach to the reference interview.

Durrance, Joan C. 1989. "Reference Success: Does the 55 Percent Rule Tell the Whole Story?" *Library Journal* 114, no. 7 (April 15): 31–36. Joan Durrance looks at several factors associated with librarian behavior on the success of the reference interview and the reference transaction. Durrance notes that accuracy is not always the best measure for determining reference success.

Durrance, Joan C. 1995. "Factors That Influence Reference Success: What Makes Questioners Willing to Return?" *Reference Librarian* no. 49/50: 243–265. Joan Durrance examines a variety of factors associated with successful reference interaction, based on a survey of library users.

Emmick, Nancy J. 1985. "Nonprofessionals on Reference Desks in Academic Libraries." In "Conflicts in Reference Services," edited by Bill Katz and Ruth A. Fraley. *The Reference Librarian* no. 12 (Spring/Summer): 149–160. Emmick's article discusses the importance of communication and referral skills if paraprofessionals are to staff a reference desk.

Flanagan, Pat, and Lisa R. Horowitz. 2000. "Exploring New Service Models: Can Consolidating Public Service Points Improve Response to Customer Needs?" *Journal of Academic Librarianship* 26, no. 5 (September): 329–338. Presents how one library combined reference and circulation desks. Especially useful are the sections describing cross training and making referrals.

Jennerich, Elaine Z., and Edward J. Jennerich. 1997. *The Reference Interview as a Creative Art.* 2nd ed. Englewood, CO: Libraries Unlimited. This book uses the theater as a metaphor to teach the reference interview.

Katz, William A. 2002. "The Reference Interview." In *Introduction to Reference Work: Volume Two: Reference Services and Reference Processes,* 8th ed., 123–140. New York: McGraw-Hill. William Katz's textbook provides another perspective on the reference interview.

Meola, Marc, and Sam Stormont. 2002. *Starting and Operating Live Virtual Reference Services: A How-To-Do-It Manual for Librarians.* New York: Neal-Schuman Publishers. In their chapter on training, Meola and Stormont provide tips on how to train for the reference interview in the virtual environment.

Reference and User Services Association Division (RUSA). Reference Services Section. Management of Reference Committee. 2004.

"Guidelines for Behavioral Performance of Reference and Information Service Providers." *Reference and User Services Quarterly* 44(Fall): 14–17. The behavioral guidelines for information service providers developed by RUSA cover five areas: approachability, interest, listening/inquiring, searching, and follow-up. The text of the guidelines is included in the appendix.

Riedling, Ann Marlow. 2000. "Great Ideas for Improving Reference Interviews." *The Book Report* 19, no. 3 (November/December): 28–29. Marlow provides tips on how school library media specialists, or anyone providing service to children and young adults, can improve communication with that user group.

Ronan, Jana. 2003. "The Reference Interview Online." *Reference & User Services Quarterly* 43, no. 1: 43–47. Jana Ronan presents the major differences between an online and in-person reference interview.

Ross, Catherine Sheldrick. 2003. "The Reference Interview: Why It Needs to Be Used in Every (Well, Almost Every) Reference Transaction." *Reference and User Services Quarterly* 43(Fall): 38–43. Ross discusses the necessity of the reference interview, some common communication problems and "negative closure."

Ross, Catherine Sheldrick, Kristi Nilsen, and Patricia Dewdney. 2002. *Conducting the Reference Interview: A How-To-Do-It Manual for Librarians*. New York: Neal-Schuman Publishers. This comprehensive manual provides more in-depth information and explanations on how to conduct a reference interview. A generous amount of exercises and tips is included.

Sutton, Ellen D., and Leslie Edmonds Holt. 1995. "The Reference Interview." In *Reference and Information Services: An Introduction*, edited by Richard E. Bopp and Linda C. Smith, 42–58. Englewood, Colorado: Libraries Unlimited.

Tyckoson, David. 2003. "Reference at Its Core: The Reference Interview." *Reference and User Services Quarterly* 43, no. 1 (Fall): 49–51. David Tyckoson reflects on the role of the reference interview in the big picture of reference service.

9 PERFORMANCE MANAGEMENT

Providing the paraprofessional with formal training is only the first step. Once the initial training is finished, the supervisor will still need to follow up with other types of less formal training so that the newly acquired skills and knowledge can be maintained. It is also important for supervisors to frequently provide their staffs with informal evaluations of performance, which can incorporate both coaching and feedback. In addition, most organizations have some sort of appraisal system in place wherein the supervisor formally evaluates the staff member's job performance. From employees' perspectives, formal and informal evaluations provide necessary feedback about their work. It is the supervisor's responsibility to make it possible for employees to improve their own performance, and thereby improve the overall service of the reference department. This chapter covers the role of standards, feedback, coaching, and the formal appraisal in reaching and maintaining desired performance levels.

MEETING PERFORMANCE STANDARDS

Performance standards for the paraprofessional should already be in place or should have been formulated during the planning stages. The supervisor should have also discussed those standards and expectations during orientation and throughout initial training. The supervisor should immediately begin regularly evaluating the employee on how well he or she is meeting those standards. It can be helpful for the supervisor to compile a checklist of those standards to ensure that he or she consistently and regularly evaluates the paraprofessional's performance. This should help the supervisor in assisting the staff member to either maintain the behavior, if he or she is performing at desired levels, or to work toward reaching standards. The supervisor can also compare those checklists over time to see how the paraprofessional is making progress and what areas need work, using the initial sheet in the series as a baseline. When grading the staff member's performance, it is important to use criteria consistent with the organization's formal performance evaluation. The supervisor should provide the paraprofessional with these performance standards, along with the criteria

Week of _____

Behavior	Poor	Fair	Average	Good	Excellent
Approachability					
Uses welcoming body language and facial expressions (eye contact, smiling, greeting users)					
Looks up from workstation; does not become engrossed in work or conversation					
Acknowledges users waiting for service					
Asks users if they need assistance, either at desks or out in library					
Interest					
Faces patron					
Demonstrates understanding of patron's needs either verbally (I see, Please tell me more) and/or nonverbally (nodding, smiling)					
Accompanies patron whenever possible					
Listening/Inquiring					
Asks open and closed questions when appropriate					
Does not interrupt					
Avoids use of library jargon					
Verifies patron's question					
Includes patron in all stages of reference transaction					
Knowledge of Resources					
Answers questions quickly and accurately using "core" reference collection and FAQs					
Able to search core group of databases					
Able to show patrons services available via library Web site					
Follow Up					
Asks patrons if question was answered					
Encourages patron to return if additional information or assistance is needed					
Understands when to refer to professional librarian					

Figure 9.1. Checklist of Model Reference Desk Behaviors

for meeting them, and the definition of what each grading category is. What does it take to get an excellent rating? What is the difference between good and fair? Taking this step will help prepare both the employee and the supervisor for the official performance appraisal. Figure 9.1 is an example of a checklist that can be used to evaluate the paraprofessional.

FEEDBACK

Employees want to know two things: (1) what is expected of them, and (2) how they are doing in their jobs. The first piece of information is provided in the performance standards or objectives. The second question is best answered by providing feedback (Geal and Johnson, 2002). It is not sufficient to provide this information at the formal performance appraisal, which could occur months or a year after the staff member has begun employment. In the true interest of developing and maintaining the paraprofessional's job performance, techniques such as feedback should be utilized far before the appraisal occurs. Performance appraisals, while a necessity, are not the best tool to manage an employee's current and future job performance. If a supervisor only provides the employee information about performance at the time of appraisal, he or she misses many opportunities to manage performance. Feedback can, and should, be given immediately, while the information is still fresh. The longer it takes a supervisor to discuss a performance issue, the larger the gap between desired and actual performance. Figure 9.2 lists some differences between appraisal and feedback. Feedback is also beneficial in that it can be a two-way

Feedback	Appraisals
Information	Evaluation or judgment
Immediate and ongoing	Occurs in intervals (semi-annual, annual, etc.)
A tool to manage present and future performance	A tool primarily used to document past performance
Verbal	Written
Two way	One way
Perceived by employees as "neutral"	Can cause fear or apprehension in employees

Source: Adapted from Lee, Christopher D. 2006. "Feedback, Not Appraisal." *HRMagazine* 51, no. 11: 111–114.

Figure 9.2. Feedback versus Appraisals

communication process that gives supervisor information about what helps or hinders an employee's performance (Lee, 2006). The frequent conversations allow the supervisor and the paraprofessional to share this information, solve performance challenges, and make necessary adjustments to reach the performance goals (McLaughlin, 2007). Utilizing feedback facilitates the collaboration to solve common problems.

The best form of feedback is informing a person that he or she has performed a certain task successfully. This practice strengthens the behavior and makes the employee more likely to repeat it. Positive feedback is also a motivator (Geal and Johnson, 2002). Most feedback will be informal, occurring as close as possible to the time of the staff member's actual performance, preferably on a daily basis. However, the supervisor should also schedule times to provide more formal feedback, especially if there is corrective or negative feedback. If there is unpleasant information to impart, there may be a tendency to delay giving informal feedback. Scheduling a formal meeting will ensure that the supervisor and employee will discuss the matter and work toward finding a solution (McLaughlin, 2007). Early on, this can take the form of daily or weekly meetings, and, as the paraprofessional grows into the job, perhaps less frequently. If negative feedback is necessary, the supervisor should consider coaching, discussed later in the chapter, to work on correcting the behavior.

Feedback is an essential part of maintaining performance levels. Feedback provides the employee with information on how he or she is doing and gives the employee a chance to work toward improvement. Moreover, the supervisor's presence and attention send the message that the supervisor cares about performance and about how the paraprofessional is contributing to the reference department.

COACHING

A more formal method to address specific performance goals and gaps is coaching. Coaching, a term usually associated with sports, is a technique utilized to help people reach their best performance and peak potential. Coaching includes feedback but also comprises drawing a person's attention to behavior, having a dialogue about that behavior, and working with a person to overcome a behavior (Metz, 2001). Coaching involves:

- Developing performance goals
- Providing focus and clear priorities
- Giving direction
- Providing encouragement
- Making suggestions for improvement

- Keeping up morale
- Providing resources
- Removing obstacles to performance
- Motivating employees (Trotta, 2006)

Coaching has several categories: The first is coaching to maintain effective performance; supervisors remind employees what is expected of them and provide regular feedback. Failure to do so can result in staff losing sight of performance goals. The second category is coaching to improve performance. Here the supervisor works with the employee to recognize and improve performance that is unsatisfactory, lagging, or poor. Finally, there is coaching to assist a staff member who is performing satisfactorily but wishes to achieve a higher level of performance (Metz, 2001).

In coaching, not only should the supervisor give positive feedback for a job well done, but he or she should meet with an individual who has performed successfully to examine what factors contributed to the success. Were there particular skills? Outside influences? It is important for the supervisor to understand what conditions made the performance possible so that it can be sustained. Likewise, when things are not done right, it is important to discuss with the employee about what the possible root of the problem is and what steps can be taken to correct the issue (Trotta, 2006). The supervisor should refrain from the assumption that the subpar performance is the fault of the employee; the reason could be factors beyond the employee's control. A number of external causes include:

> **Benefits of Coaching**
>
> - Results oriented.
> - Stresses continual learning.
> - Helps individuals develop goals that are in line with the goals of the library.
> - Offers guidance in overcoming personality traits and/ or skill deficits that might hinder reaching goals. (Trotta, 2006, p. 95)

- Poor policies and procedures
- Ineffective communication about performance standards
- Ineffective training
- Inadequate equipment
- Faulty hiring (the employee does not possess the necessary knowledge, skills, or attitudes)

But poor performance can also be the employee's fault. Some causes are:

- Failure to accept one or more performance standards
- Poor relationships with coworkers
- Unhappiness with supervisor
- Unwillingness to work to improve performance
- Intrusion of personal issues into work life

The supervisor must, either alone or with the employee, remove barriers to meeting performance goals (Evans, 2004). When working with the staff member to correct behavior, it is important that the tone is positive.

I	Take responsibility using **I**: "I noticed that you seem uncomfortable conducting a reference interview."
D	**Describe** what was observed: "I noticed that you take each patron's request at face value."
E	**Elicit** their opinion: "What do you think? Do you agree with what I observed?"
A	Suggest a course of **Action**: "You might try acknowledging what they ask for and asking them to elaborate 'Yes, we have a lot of books about dogs. Could you please tell me more about what you are looking for so that I can take you directly to what you need?'"

Source: Adapted from Voyles, Jeanne F., and Carol A. Friesen. "Coaching for Results." In *Staff Development: A Practical Guide.* 3rd ed., edited by Elizabeth Fuseler Avery, Terry Dahlin, and Deborah A. Carver, 83–87. Chicago and London: American Library Association, 2001.

Figure 9.3. The IDEA Method for Providing Constructive Feedback

Keeping things as optimistic as possible will yield a better response from the employee; scolding or yelling will simply make the employee defensive. When discussing poor or subpar performance, the supervisor should also focus on the specific situations and behaviors rather than personality traits. In order to effectively work together to solve performance problems or reach performance goals, the supervisor should ask the paraprofessional questions and listen to the responses, offering suggestions and support. The supervisor should make it clear that change is needed and have the paraprofessional talk about how he or she plans to improve. The supervisor and employee should set outcomes and time lines for improvement (McLaughlin, 2007). The idea is to contribute, not criticize. The coaching process should help the employee understand standards and expectations and how to be successful (Metz, 2001). Figure 9.3 provides an example of how to provide constructive feedback.

There are several stages of coaching. The first coaching session involves a meeting to define an issue or an outcome. Before the meeting, the supervisor should take the time to describe the issue and what the desired outcome is, devise possible approaches, develop a plan of action, and set criteria for evaluation. During the meeting the supervisor and paraprofessional should come to a decision about what direction to pursue. Each person should determine if additional training is needed, identify barriers to performance, and designate time lines and deadlines. Both parties will need to have clear expectations and have a good understanding of what the steps are to achieve the desired goal (Voyles and Friesen, 2001). Figure 9.4 describes this process.

An important part of coaching is for the supervisor to be a role model, demonstrating the desired behaviors and leading by example. Failure to do so could undermine any coaching effort. A supervisor's performance and behavior at the reference desk and elsewhere will be noticed and emulated by staff members. If the supervisor does not set an example, the paraprofessional may believe the manager has a "do as I do, not as I say" attitude.

Outcome: Improve the paraprofessional's reference interview.

Barriers: Employee is unclear about difference between open and closed questions. Employee also feels that he or she is disrespectful of patron when he does not take initial request at face value.

Time line: Supervisor and paraprofessional schedule time together at reference desk three times per week for the next six months.

Steps:

- Supervisor will provide staff member with examples of open and closed questions. Supervisor will also discuss techniques for getting patrons to elaborate on their information needs.
- Paraprofessional will shadow supervisor at reference desk. Supervisor will deconstruct successful reference interview he or she has conducted.
- Paraprofessional will practice using open and closed questions at reference desk.
- Supervisor will provide positive feedback when needed and meet with paraprofessional once a week to discuss progress, opportunities, and challenges.

Deadline: In six months, paraprofessional will demonstrate improved reference interviewing skills.

Figure 9.4. Coaching for the Reference Interview

It is important to remember that "actions speak louder than words," no matter how often policies and standards are articulated. Supervisors must demonstrate enthusiasm and passion about work (Trotta, 2006).

Coaching is an action-oriented approach to managing performance. This must be a two-way communication process. The supervisor's role is to help the employee develop the necessary behaviors and skills necessary to meet performance standards. The staff member, in turn, should make an effort to develop those skills and provide feedback on problems and barriers to performance. Together, the employee and the supervisor can maintain and improve performance.

FORMAL EVALUATION

The supervisor will also evaluate the paraprofessional's performance during the formal appraisal. Performance appraisals are an official written record of an employee's job performance and accomplishments and take place once or twice a year. How to conduct an appraisal is beyond the scope of this work and is better covered in other resources; however, the formal appraisal plays a role in managing the paraprofessional's performance.

The performance evaluation is the time to officially document how the employee is doing in the job and to set up goals for growth and improvement. The appraisal also gives the staff member the opportunity to officially raise concerns he or she may have. At this point, what is discussed should be a mere formality; nothing should come as a surprise to the employee. The performance appraisal should merely continue what has been discussed during feedback and/or coaching. Because this is a formal procedure, serves as a permanent record, and goes beyond the department, there are some things for the supervisor to keep in mind.

What is written down in the formal appraisal should be consistent with what has been documented during the informal processes for performance management. If the paraprofessional is not performing up to standards, the appraisal should reflect this. Because this process is more official and a matter of permanent record, the supervisor should be aware that the employee could be nervous and therefore not as willing to discuss unsatisfactory performance, voice concerns or set goals. It is important to rate each task separately. If the paraprofessional is knowledgeable about sources but has an unpleasant desk demeanor, he or she should receive a high mark and a low mark, accordingly. Personal feelings should not factor into how an employee is rated. Also, even if performance feedback, goal setting, and indentifying training needs occurred prior to the performance appraisal, these should still be discussed and officially documented.

It is important to maintain records of employee performance throughout the rating period, noting various aspects of work performance. A review of the training objectives can be useful to see how much the paraprofessional has learned. The weekly checklists can be consulted to see what sort of progress was made. Notes from coaching and counseling sessions may be used as reminders of past problems or accomplishments that can be mentioned in an evaluation. This can be particularly crucial if performance was poor, as it is best to have a basis when confronting subpar performance (Metz, 2001).

Managing performance is an ongoing activity. Supervisors must work with employees to ensure that knowledge and skills imparted in training are kept and that attitudes necessary to successful performance are developed. Feedback and coaching are methods that will help improve, maintain or boost performance; the performance appraisal officially documents these efforts. Good supervisors should utilize these varying techniques, as situations warrant, to evaluate the paraprofessional's work, maintain and improve performance, and maximize the effectiveness of the department's work.

REFERENCES

Evans, G. Edward. 2004. *Performance Management and Appraisal: A How-To-Do-It Manual for Librarians*. New York: Neal-Schuman Publishers. While mostly devoted to the business of the formal performance appraisal, Evans discusses the role of coaching in having staff perform at its best.

Geal, Mandy, and Barry Johnson. 2002. "Management Performance: A Glimpse of the Blindingly Obvious." *Training Journal* (October): 24–27. Available: www.proquest.com/. Accessed: June 16, 2008. Geal and Johnson list effective performance management techniques, including feedback, meetings, and walking the floor.

Lee, Christopher D. 2006. "Feedback, Not Appraisal." *HRMagazine* 51, no. 11: 111–114. Lee argues against using the formal performance appraisal as the sole tool for managing performance and discusses the pros of using feedback and coaching.

McLaughlin, Peter. 2007. "Giving Good Feedback." *Supervision* 68, no. 2: 7–8. McLaughlin presents the importance of providing feedback and lists seven tips on how to do it well.

Metz, Ruth F. 2001. *Coaching in the Library: A Management Strategy for Achieving Excellence.* Chicago and London: American Library Association. This book is devoted entirely to the concept of coaching in the library. It provides an overview of coaching, describes an effective coach, and has chapters devoted to coaching individuals, teams, leaders, and managers.

Trotta, Marcia. 2006. *Supervising Staff: A How-To-Do-It Manual for Librarians.* New York: Neal-Schuman Publishers. In her chapter "Mentoring and Coaching Staff," Trotta provides guidance to supervisors who wish to coach.

Voyles, Jeanne F., and Carol A. Friesen. 2001. "Coaching for Results." In *Staff Development: A Practical Guide.* 3rd ed., edited by Elizabeth Fuseler Avery, Terry Dahlin, and Deborah A. Carver, 83–87. Chicago and London: American Library Association. For those who need a quick introduction to coaching in the library, this chapter is a good place to start.

10 EVALUATION AND REVISION OF TRAINING

A good deal of training literature still refers to Don Kirkpatricks's four levels of evaluation.

- Reaction—Were trainees satisfied with the program?
- Learning—What knowledge, skills and attitudes did the trainees acquire?
- Behavior—Did the training change the trainee's behavior that improves job performance?
- Results—Did the training produce the desired results? (Birnbrauer, 1987, p. 53)

It is important to evaluate the training provided to the paraprofessional. Evaluation provides the means by which the success of the training program can be judged (Trotta, 1995). Evaluation of training consists of several objectives (Allan, 2003):

- To provide feedback on the content and the delivery of the training so that successful elements can be retained and less effective portions can be modified or dropped
- To gauge what the trainee has learned
- To determine whether changes in the paraprofessional's job performance are tied to the training
- To gauge the effectiveness and efficiency of the training
- To ensure that the training is aligned with library goals

The supervisor should gather information on the following to comprehensively evaluate the training: trainee reaction, trainee performance, training delivery and content, and trainer strengths and weaknesses, and costs (Creth, 1986). Four segments (sometimes referred to as "levels") should be used for this process. These are reaction, learning, behavior, and results. It is not enough to use one method, as each segment measures different things. For each segment of evaluation, the library will need to determine benchmarks for success. The time to do this is during the planning stages, as the library determines what it hopes to accomplish by using paraprofessionals, decides what the training needs are, sets performance expectations, and establishes the criteria for the written training objectives. As the planning process (covered in greater detail in Chapter 2) unfolds, the supervisor should be asking, "What should the trainee have learned?" and "What are the desired results from training?" All of these things should be factored into the benchmarks for training success. Once the information about the training is gathered, the supervisor will have to decide what the next steps are. Was the training worth the time and effort? Are there more efficient means by which the paraprofessional can learn what he or she needs to know? If the library decides to continue with training, what will be retained and what will be discarded (Creth, 1986)?

Three ways to elicit reactions from training participants:

- Have participants fill out a questionnaire.
- Ask each participant to write down one key thing he or she learned and one thing they would like to see changed.
- Ask participants to share what they liked and what they didn't like about the training. (adapted from Allan, 2003, pp. 209–210)

This chapter covers the following aspects of the evaluation and revision of training programs: the reaction survey, performance testing, observation of behavior, impact on the library and revision of training.

REACTION

The first "level" of evaluation is trainee reaction. How did the employee feel about the content and delivery of the training? A common tool to gauge the reaction to training is a questionnaire with a method of rating, such as a Likert scale (Woodard, 1995). Since the reaction is how people feel when they leave the session, it is important to have questions that are appropriate to ask immediately following the training (Allan, 2003). Examples of questions include:

- Was the content too easy or too difficult?
- Was the amount of material presented appropriate? (Was more or less needed?)
- Was there time to practice?
- Was the trainer supportive?
- Was the environment conducive to asking questions?
- Were the training materials useful?
- Was anything omitted?
- What could be done to improve the training process?

In short, was the training valuable to the participant (Creth, 1986)? The paraprofessional should be able to judge if the pace of the session was appropriate, if there was enough time to practice, whether questions were encouraged, etc. The employee should also be able to indicate whether he or she feels more confident about doing his or her job following the training (Allen, 2003). There should also be questions about the facilities and the training space; these factors can impact the perception—and success—of training. Comfortable space and adequate facilities are conducive to learning (Trotta, 1995). The form should also provide space for additional comments. A sample questionnaire is provided in Figure 10.1.

In addition to the initial reaction survey, there should be an ongoing discussion about the longer-term reaction and training needs. As the employee gains more experience at the reference desk, he or she will better be able to judge the continuing effectiveness of the training. For example, following a training workshop on the reference interview, the paraprofessional may have indicated that he or she felt better about conducting a reference interview; however, after the employee has spent more time

Please help us improve our Reference Training Program by filling out this form. Your responses to this survey will help the reference department to identify strengths and weaknesses in the Reference Assistant Training Program. Your answers will be confidential and will not affect your evaluation.

Please check a box to indicate your rating.

1 = strongly disagree; 2 = somewhat disagree; 3 = no opinion; 4 = somewhat agree; 5 = strongly agree

	1	2	3	4	5
The pace of instruction was appropriate for me					
The instructions were clear and understandable					
I was able to understand what was presented					
The length of the session was appropriate					
The session was well-organized					
The handouts were helpful					
There was adequate time for hands-on practice					
The practice questions were helpful and related to my job					
The training session was useful and will help me do my job better					
There was enough time to ask questions					
The trainer was well-prepared					
The trainer was enthusiastic					
The trainer encouraged my questions and answered them					
The space for training was satisfactory					
The equipment functioned properly					

1. What would you keep the same about the session?

2. What would you change about the session?

3. Are there any other comments you would like to add?

Figure 10.1 Training Rating Form

actually interacting with patrons and determining information needs, the conclusion may be that ongoing coaching is a better means for training. Formal feedback meetings and/or coaching sessions (discussed in greater detail in Chapter 6) are excellent opportunities to further discuss the training. The supervisor should ask the paraprofessional for about training content that was presented that was both necessary and unnecessary for job performance, in what areas the staff member feels more training is needed, and for a general opinion of the training program. The supervisor should encourage the employee to be as honest as possible. If the paraprofessional indicates that most of what he or she learned was learned while on the reference desk, the supervisor may decide that future training sessions are not worth the time, resources, and effort.

LEARNING

The second level of evaluation is learning; what has the paraprofessional learned during the training? For example, a goal is that the paraprofessional should be able to use the online catalog to assist patrons; the objective is that given a catalog record, the paraprofessional will be able to correctly identify all information in the record. This objective contains two benchmarks: the quantity is "all information" and the quality is "error free." Following the training, is the paraprofessional able to do to this? A reaction survey will not provide this information. One method to see what the employee learned during training is to use a pretest and a posttest. Using this method will help determine if the paraprofessional has acquired the necessary knowledge, skills, and attitudes (Woodard, 1995). A pretest would have been administered to see what areas needed training. By having the paraprofessional repeat the test following the training, the supervisor can measure how much more the paraprofessional has learned and whether additional training is required. (A sample pretest for the online catalog is provided in Chapter 3.) Because the paraprofessional has been acquiring knowledge and skills by means other than training (e.g., observing at the reference desk), the posttest should focus on those sources covered by the training program. In order for the posttest to provide the most precise possible measure of learning, the paraprofessional should not be forewarned about the test. This stage of evaluation will help determine if the training objectives were met. If the staff member can meet the objectives, then apparently the training was successful. If the paraprofessional is unable to meet the criteria for success (e.g., he or she cannot correctly identify the all the information in the catalog record), it is important to determine why. Is the measurement of the objective unrealistic? Is the training to blame? Or is the paraprofessional simply incapable of performing as expected?

The posttest can also be given much later, after the conclusion of training, to determine if the employee remembers what he or she was taught and if he or she is using the information on the job. If the staff member provides incorrect answers to a considerable number of questions in one subject area, this may indicate that those sources are rarely utilized on the job or that the training was ineffective or insufficient. If this occurs, these areas should be discussed with the paraprofessional to determine if the sources are used often enough to warrant further inclusion in the training program.

BEHAVIOR

There is a difference between being able to perform tasks in a training session or during a test and performing them on the job (Woodard, 1995). In addition, some desired traits (approachability or demonstrating interest) or skills (conducting a reference interview) do not lend themselves to testing. The supervisor should try to find time to observe the paraprofessional at the reference desk. Is the paraprofessional able to search successfully? Can he or she use reference sources effectively? Does he or she interact comfortably with the patrons? If the paraprofessional is not making adequate progress in these areas, the effectiveness of the training may need to be reevaluated. The supervisor should also consult with other staff members who might also have observations about the staff member's performance and behavior. A helpful tool to use during observation is the Checklist of Reference Skills (Figure 9.1).

RESULTS

What are the overall results from training? What is the benefit to the organization? It can be helpful to revisit the original reasons behind the decision to have paraprofessionals staff the reference desk and determine whether those goals being met (Todaro, 2001). Is staff being used more efficiently? Is the library able to add or maintain services while maintaining standards? This can be done by a discussion among library decision makers. To determine the impact of training on library service to patrons, libraries can administer user surveys. However, it is difficult to link training and overall library performance (Allan, 2003). Training also requires time and effort. Every hour that the paraprofessional is at training is an hour that the paraprofessional is not at the reference desk; the process also takes up the time of the trainer. The library must answer the question: Was the training a worthwhile effort? The library may decide that it cannot spare the employee

Why evaluate?

- To determine whether trainee needs have been met
- To determine whether the library's needs have been met
- To adapt the training program if it is not meeting the above needs (Trotta, 1995, p. 92)

Learning is an ongoing process. In addition to the initial and subsequent in-house training, there may be continuing education opportunities that the paraprofessional can take advantage of. The library will need to decide if staffing and workflow will permit the paraprofessional to attend outside workshops and conferences. There are national and statewide conferences specifically aimed at paraprofessionals, which provide good educational and networking opportunities and the chance for paraprofessionals to learn from one another. The American Library Association's Library Support Staff Interest Roundtable provides a comprehensive list of resources: Available online: www.ala.org/ala/lssirt/lssirtresources/resourcelinks.cfm

and the trainer and therefore will have to revisit how the training will be acquired on the job. If, after the training, the paraprofessional does not meet performance standards, the amount of training may have been inadequate. The library will ultimately make up for this time in retraining, inefficient service to patrons, or both. The library should consider the cost of materials as well as staff time used in planning for and conducting the training. The library then needs to compare these costs to the value of using paraprofessionals at the reference desk to determine what changes can be made to improve the library's return on its investment.

REVISION OF TRAINING

One goal of evaluation is to determine what changes to the training, if any, are required. Libraries are changing rapidly with the introduction of new technologies, services, and sources. The training program will need to keep pace with the change. The supervisor should note things such as new tools, new sources, and new services, and incorporate the appropriate changes into the training. When revising the training modules, it is important to make sure that the sources covered are still relevant. The source may no longer be used, or a new edition or an online version may be available. Do the practice questions reflect the types of queries patrons have? The answers to the questions should be verified.

The supervisor should consult the reaction survey, notes from meetings where training was discussed with the paraprofessional, results from the testing, and notes from any observation. The supervisor should note any suggestions the employee had on what was most helpful and what was unnecessary. The supervisor may determine that some training works in sessions and modules (such as how to search a database or use print resources) but that behavioral training is better achieved by a method such as coaching and feedback. The supervisor may also decide to use different people for training. Perhaps the paraprofessional needs more time on database searching rather than being trained on print reference sources. Once the supervisor has pinpointed methods, content, and personnel that need to be modified, then he or she can begin to make changes in anticipation for the next trainee.

Training is a process, not a one-time event. The evaluation and revision is just a part of a cycle. With the information and experience gained from training the first paraprofessional or group of paraprofessionals, it is time to return to Chapter 2 and begin the planning process again. Each time the training process will be easier because the department manual, modules, and checklists will be available to use.

REFERENCES

Allan, Barbara. (Moran, Barbara, North American editor). 2003. *Training Skills for Library Staff*. Lanham, MD: Scarecrow Press. The chapter "Evaluating Training Sessions" has information on the four "levels" of evaluation and also provides examples adapted from the training literature.

Birnbrauer, Herman. 1987. "Evaluation Techniques that Work." *Training & Development Journal* 41, no. 7: 53.

Creth, Shelia D. 1986. *Effective On-the-Job Training*. Chicago and London: American Library Association. The chapter "Evaluation of Training" provides information on who evaluates, what, how and when to evaluate, and what to do with the information provided by the evaluation of training.

Todaro, Julie. 2001. "Evaluating Your Program." In *Staff Development: A Practical Guide*. 3rd Edition, edited by Elizabeth Fuseler Avery, Terry Dahlin, and Deborah A. Carver, 155–161. Chicago and London: American Library Association. Julie Todaro provides an overview of how to evaluate a training program.

Trotta, Marcia. 1995. *Successful Staff Development: A How-To-Do-It Manual*. New York and London: Neal-Schuman Publishers. In her chapter "Evaluating Staff Performance" Trotta has included a section on the need to evaluate training.

Woodard, Beth S. 1995. "Reference Training." In *The Reference Assessment Manual*. Compiled and edited by the Evaluation and Adults Services Committee Management and Operations of Public Services Section, Reference and Adult Services Division (RASD), American Library Association, 67–75. Ann Arbor, MI: The Pieran Press. Woodard provides an overview of research in the area of the evaluation of reference training, thereby summarizing many of the theories and ideas.

APPENDIX
GUIDELINES FOR BEHAVIORAL PERFORMANCE OF REFERENCE AND INFORMATION SERVICE PROVIDERS

(From the American Library Association, Reference and User Services Association Division. Revised by MOUSS Management of Reference Committee and approved by the ALA and the RUSA Board of Directors, June 2004.)

1.0 APPROACHABILITY

In order to have a successful reference transaction, patrons must be able to identify that a reference librarian is available to provide assistance and also must feel comfortable in going to that person for help. In remote environments, this also means placing contact information for chat, e-mail, telephone, and other services in prominent locations, to make them obvious and welcoming to patrons. Approachability behaviors, such as the initial verbal and nonverbal responses of the librarian, will set the tone for the entire communication process, and will influence the depth and level of interaction between the staff and the patrons. At this stage in the process, the behaviors exhibited by the staff member should serve to welcome the patrons and to place them at ease. The librarian's role in the communications process is to make the patrons feel comfortable in a situation that may be perceived as intimidating, risky, confusing, and overwhelming.

To be approachable, the librarian:

GENERAL

1.1 Establishes a "reference presence" wherever patrons look for it. This includes having Reference Services in a highly visible location and using proper signage (both in the library and on the library's Web site) to indicate the location, hours, and availability of in-person and remote help or assistance.

1.2 Is poised and ready to engage approaching patrons. The librarian is aware of the need to stop all other activities when patrons approach and focus attention on the patrons' needs.

1.3 Acknowledges others waiting for service.

    1.3.1 Employs a system of question triage to identify what types of questions the patrons have when more than two patrons are waiting. Frequently asked questions, brief informational questions, directional questions, and referrals can be answered quickly, allowing more time to devote to in-depth reference questions.

IN PERSON

1.4 Establishes initial eye contact with patrons, and acknowledges the presence of patrons through smiling and attentive and welcoming body language.

1.5 Acknowledges patrons through the use of a friendly greeting to initiate conversation, and by standing up, moving forward, or moving closer to them.

1.6 Remains visible to patrons as much as possible.

1.7 Roves through the reference area offering assistance whenever possible. Librarians should make themselves available to patrons by offering assistance at their point of need rather than waiting for patrons to come to the reference desk. To rove successfully, the librarian should:

    1.7.1 Be mobile. Get the patrons started on the initial steps of their search, then move on to other patrons.

    1.7.2 Address the patrons before addressing their computer screen. Patrons are more likely to confide in librarians and discuss their needs if they do not perceive the librarians as "policing" the area.

    1.7.3 Approach patrons and offer assistance with lines such as, "Are you finding what you need?" "Can I help you with anything?" or "How is your search going?"

    1.7.4 Check back on the patron's progress after helping him or her start a search.

    1.7.5 If the reference desk has been left unattended, check back periodically to see if there are patrons waiting for assistance there.

REMOTE

1.8 Should provide prominent, jargon-free links to all forms of reference services from the *home page* of the library's Web site, and throughout the site wherever research assistance may be sought out. The Web should be used to make reference services easy to find and convenient.

2.0 INTEREST

A successful librarian must demonstrate a high degree of interest in the reference transaction. While not every query will contain stimulating intellectual challenges, the librarian should be interested in each patron's informational need and should be committed to providing the most effective assistance. Librarians who demonstrate a high level of interest in the inquiries of their patrons will generate a higher level of satisfaction among users. To demonstrate interest, the librarian:

GENERAL

2.1 Faces the patron when speaking and listening.

2.2 Focuses attention on the patrons.

IN PERSON

2.3 Faces patrons when speaking and listening.

2.4 Maintains or reestablishes eye contact with patrons throughout the transaction.

2.5 Signals an understanding of patrons' needs through verbal or nonverbal confirmation, such as nodding of the head or brief comments or questions.

REMOTE

2.6 Maintains or reestablishes "word contact" with the patron in text-based environments by sending written or prepared prompts, etc., to convey interest in the patron's question.

2.7 Acknowledges user e-mail questions in a timely manner.

2.8 States question-answering procedures and policies clearly in an accessible place on the Web. This should indicate question scope, types of answers provided, and expected turnaround time.

3.0 LISTENING/INQUIRING

The reference interview is the heart of the reference transaction and is crucial to the success of the process. The librarian must be effective in identifying the patron's information needs and must do so in a manner that keeps patrons at ease. Strong listening and questioning skills are necessary for a positive interaction. As a good communicator, the librarian:

GENERAL

3.1 Communicates in a receptive, cordial, and encouraging manner.

3.2 Uses a tone of voice and/or written language appropriate to the nature of the transaction.

3.3 Allows the patrons to state fully their information need in their own words before responding.

3.4 Identifies the goals or objectives of the user's research, when appropriate.

3.5 Rephrases the question or request and asks for confirmation to ensure that it is understood.

3.6 Seeks to clarify confusing terminology and avoids excessive jargon.

3.7 Uses open-ended questioning techniques to encourage patrons to expand on the request or present additional information. Some examples of such questions include:

- Please tell me more about your topic.

- What additional information can you give me?

- How much information do you need?

3.8 Uses closed and/or clarifying questions to refine the search query. Some examples of clarifying questions are:

- What have you already found?

- What type of information do you need (books, articles, etc.)?
- Do you need current or historical information?

3.9 Maintains objectivity and does not interject value judgments about subject matter or the nature of the question into the transaction.

REMOTE

3.10 Uses reference interviews or Web forms to gather as much information as possible without compromising user privacy.

4.0 SEARCHING

The search process is the portion of the transaction in which behavior and accuracy intersect. Without an effective search, not only is the desired information unlikely to be found, but patrons may become discouraged as well. Yet many of the aspects of searching that lead to accurate results are still dependent on the behavior of the librarian. As an effective searcher, the librarian:

GENERAL

4.1 Finds out what patrons have already tried, and encourages patrons to contribute ideas.

4.2 Constructs a competent and complete search strategy. This involves:
- Selecting search terms that are most related to the information desired.
- Verifying spelling and other possible factual errors in the original query.
- Identifying sources appropriate to the patron's need that have the highest probability of containing information relevant to the patron's query.

4.3 Explains the search strategy and sequence to the patrons, as well as the sources to be used.

4.4 Attempts to conduct the search within the patron's allotted time frame.

4.5   Explains how to use sources when appropriate.

4.6   Works with the patrons to narrow or broaden the topic when too little or too much information is identified.

4.7   Asks the patron if additional information is needed after an initial result is found.

4.8   Recognizes when to refer patron to a more appropriate guide, database, library, librarian, or other resource.

4.9   Offers pointers, detailed search paths (including complete URLs), and names of resources used to find the answer, so that patrons can learn to answer similar questions on their own.

IN PERSON

4.10   Accompanies the patron in the search (at least in the initial stages of the search process).

REMOTE

4.11   Uses appropriate technology (such as co-browsing, scanning, faxing, etc.) to help guide patrons through library resources, when possible.

5.0 FOLLOW-UP

The reference transaction does not end when the librarian leaves the patron. The librarian is responsible for determining if the patron is satisfied with the results of the search, and is also responsible for referring the patron to other sources, even when those sources are not available in the local library. For successful follow-up, the librarian:

GENERAL

5.1 Asks patrons if their questions have been completely answered.

5.2 Encourages the patrons to return if they have further questions by making a statement such as "If you don't find what you are looking for, please come back and we'll try something else."

5.3 Roving (see 1.7) is an excellent technique for follow-up.

5.4 Consults other librarians or experts in the field when additional subject expertise is needed.

5.5 Makes patron aware of other appropriate reference services (e-mail, etc.).

5.6 Makes arrangements, when appropriate, with the patron to research a question even after the reference transaction has been completed.

5.7 Refers the patron to other sources or institutions when the query cannot be answered to the satisfaction of the patron.

5.8 Facilitates the process of referring patrons to another library or information agency through activities such as calling ahead, providing direction and instructions, and providing the library and the patrons with as much information as possible about the amount of information required, and sources already consulted.

5.9 Takes care not to end the reference interview prematurely.

REMOTE

5.9 Suggests that the patron visit or call the library when appropriate.

General: Guidelines that can be applied in any type of reference interaction, including both in-person and remote transactions.

In Person: Additional guidelines that are specific to face-to-face encounters, and make the most sense in this context.

Remote: Additional guidelines that are specific to reference encounters by telephone, e-mail, chat, etc., where traditional visual and nonverbal cues do not exist.

Note: The term *librarian* in this document applies to all who provide reference and informational services directly to library users.

GLOSSARY

abstract: A short summary describing the main idea or content of a work such as an article, book, or dissertation.

Boolean searching: A system where terms (AND, OR, and NOT) are used in computer searching to narrow or broaden a search. AND narrows a search; OR broadens a search; NOT excludes search term(s).

call number: A unique number assigned to library materials for shelving. A call number of a book tells exactly where a book is located on the shelf. It also groups together books with a similar subject on the shelf.

circulating collection: Materials that can be checked out and taken from the library.

citation: The basic information about a book or article that is used to identify that book or article. Can include author, title, date, volume, issue, pages, and place of publication.

database: A database is an organized collection of information that is organized in an electronic format that can be searched electronically.

e-book: A book that is in electronic format only.

e-journal: Full-text journals available in online format.

e-reserves: Some reserve materials (book chapters and articles, NOT entire books) stored electronically on the library Web site under both the course number and the instructors name. *See also* RESERVES.

federated search: A search process and tool that allows patrons to simultaneously search multiple databases, including the online catalog if desired, using a single interface.

full-text: Full-text means that the entire article is available in the database.

government document: A document issued by a government. Government documents include publications from states, the federal government, or international organizations such as the United Nations. *See also* SUDOC.

hold: A method of electronically requesting a book that is checked out. The patron will be notified when the book is returned. *See also* RECALL.

ILL: An acronym for interlibrary loan, which is a method for a libraries to borrow and lend materials to one another.

ISBN: An acronym for International Standard Book Number. This is a ten- or thirteen-digit (ISBN 13) number that is a unique identifying number for books.

ISSN: International Standard Serial Number. This is a unique eight-digit number to identify serials.

journal: A publication that contains scholarly articles written either by professors, researchers, or experts in a subject area. *See also* MAGAZINE; PERIODICAL; SERIAL.

link resolver: A tool that, if the full text of an article is not available in one database, allows a person to click on a link to another database if the full text of the article is available in that other database.

magazine: A serial that is intended for the general public. *See also* JOURNAL; PERIODICAL; SERIAL.

online catalog: The online catalog is a database of the materials (books, newspapers, magazines and journals, documents but NOT articles) the library owns.

OPAC: Acronym for Online Public Access Catalog. *See also* ONLINE CATALOG.

peer-reviewed: A process that articles in many scholarly journals go through before publication. Once an article is submitted for publication, it is sent to an editorial board for evaluation by an expert in that field. The submitted article must receive the approval of the editorial board before it is published. Peer-reviewed journals may also be called refereed journals.

periodical: An item published or issued usually on a regular basis, e.g., daily, weekly, monthly, or quarterly. Journals, magazines, and newspapers are all periodicals. *See also* JOURNAL; MAGAZINE; SERIAL.

recall: A method of electronically requesting a book that is checked out The person who has the book checked out has seven days to return the book, and the patron who wants the book will be notified the book is returned. *See also* HOLD.

reference collection: Material designed to be consulted for brief items of information such as facts, statistics, background information, etc. This material generally does not circulate. Examples include encyclopedias, dictionaries, and almanacs.

reference desk: The location in the library where patrons can ask for help in finding information, using the library's resources, or doing research.

renew: The process of extending the time that material can be borrowed. This can be done electronically or in person.

request: A method of electronically requesting a book that is kept in off-site storage.

reserve: Materials, such as articles and books, that instructors put aside for students to check out for a limited time. Some reserve materials (book chapters and articles, NOT entire books) are available electronically as e-reserves. *See also* E-RESERVE.

search term: A word or phrase that is typed into the search box of the library catalog or other database in order to find information.

serial: A library term for periodical. *See also* JOURNAL; MAGAZINE; PERIODICAL.

SuDoc: Superintendent of Documents Classification. A string of letters and numbers used to identify and label publications issued by the United States federal government. The letters beginning each SuDoc classification number refer to the government agency responsible for the publication.

subject: In order to organize a collection of information, the articles in the database are given subject headings. Subject headings are standardized terms that describe the book or article.

BIBLIOGRAPHY

Allan, Barbara. (Moran, Barbara, North American editor). 2003. *Training Skills for Library Staff*. Lanham, MD. Metuchen, NJ: Scarecrow Press.

Allegri, Francesca, and Martha Bedard. 2006. "Lessons Learned from Single Service Point Implementations." *Medical Reference Services Quarterly* 25, no. 2 (Summer): 31–47.

Avery, Elizabeth Fuseler, Terry Dahlin, and Deborah A. Carver. 2001. *Staff Development: A Practical Guide*. 3rd ed. Chicago and London: American Library Association.

Badke, William. 2008. "What to Do with Wikipedia." *Online* 32, no. 2 (March/April): 48–50.

Barclay, Kevin. 2004. "Public Library Reference Desk: Less Is More." *OLA Q* 10, no. 2/3 (Fall): 2–4.

Belcastro, Patricia. 1998. *Evaluating Library Staff: A Performance Appraisal System*. Chicago: American Library Association.

Bell, Steven J. 2007. "Who Needs a Reference Desk?" *Library Issues* 27, no. 6 (July): 1–4.

Benefiel, Candace R., Jeannie P. Miller, and Diana Ramirez. 1997. "Baseline Subject Competencies for the Academic Reference Desk." *Reference Services Review* 25, no. 1: 83–93.

Berinstein, Paula. 2006. "Wikipedia and Britannica." *Searcher* 14, no. 3 (March): 16–26.

Berkow, Ellen, and Betty Morganstern. 1990. "Getting to the Core: Training Librarians in Basic Reference Tools." *Reference Librarian* no. 30: 191–206.

Berwind, Anne May. 1991. "Orientation for the Reference Desk." *Reference Services Review* 19(Fall): 51–54, 70.

Birkmeyer, Carl. 2004. "Conducting the Reference Interview." Videodisc. Library Video Network.

Boorkman, Jo Anne, Jeffrey T. Huber, and Fred W. Roper. 2004. *Introduction to Reference Sources in the Health Sciences*. 4th ed. New York: Neal-Schuman Publishers.

Bopp, Richard E., and Linda C. Smith, eds. 2001. *Reference and Information Services*. 3rd ed. Englewood, CO: Libraries Unlimited.

Borin, Jacqueline. 2001 "Training, Supervising, and Evaluating Student Information Assistants." *The Reference Librarian* no. 72: 195–206.

Boyer, Laura M., and William C. Theimer, Jr. 1975. "The Use and Training of Nonprofessional Personnel at Reference Desks in Selected College and University Libraries." *College & Research Libraries* 36, no. 3 (May): 193–200.

Bracke, Marianne Stowell, Michael Brewer, Robyn Huff-Eibl, Daniel R. Lee, Robert Mitchell, and Michael Ray. 2007. "Finding Information in a New Landscape: Developing New Service and Staffing Models for Mediated Information Services." *College & Research Libraries* 68, no. 3 (May): 248–267.

Brandt, D. Scott. 2002. *Teaching Technology: A How-To-Do-It Manual for Librarians*. New York: Neal-Schuman Publishers.

Brandys, Barbara, Joan Daghita, and Susan Whitmore. 2002. "Raising the Bar or Training Library Technicians to Assume Reference Responsibilities." In SLA 2002: Putting Knowledge to Work. Papers Presented at the Special Libraries Association Conference (Los Angeles, California, June 9–12, 2002).

Burgett, Shelly Wood. 2006. "If It Isn't Written, It Doesn't Exist: Creating a Library Policy Manual." In *It's All About Student Learning: Managing Community and Other Libraries in the 21st Century,* edited by David R. Dowell and Gerard B. McCabe, 253–260. Westport, CT: Libraries Unlimited.

Cassell, Kay Ann, and Uma Hiremath. 2004. "Answering Questions About Anything and Everything—Encyclopedias." In *Reference and Information Services in the 21st Century: An Introduction,* 69–92. New York: Neal-Schuman Publishers.

Cassell, Kay Ann, and Uma Hiremath. 2004. "Answering Questions About Governments—Government Information Sources." In *Reference and Information Services in the 21st Century: An Introduction,* 213–230. New York: Neal-Schuman Publishers.

Cassell, Kay Ann, and Uma Hiremath. 2004. "Answering Questions About Health, Law, and Business—Special Guidelines and Sources." In *Reference and Information Services in the 21st Century: An Introduction,* 155–182. New York: Neal-Schuman Publishers.

Cervone, Frank. 2007. "Federated Searching: Today, Tomorrow and the Future(?)" *Serials* 20, no. 1: 67–70.

"Checklist for New Employee Orientation." 2000. *Library Personnel News* 13, no. 1–2 (Spring/Summer): 15–16.

Cohn, John M., and Ann L. Kelsey. 2005. *Staffing the Modern Library: A How-To-Do-It Manual*. New York: Neal-Schuman Publishers.

Courtois, Martin P., and Lori A. Goetsch. 1984. "Use of Nonprofessionals at Reference Desks." *College & Research Libraries* 45, no. 5 (September): 385–391.

Crawford, Holly. 2001. "Encyclopedias." In *Reference and Information Services*. 3rd ed., edited by Richard E. Bopp and Linda C. Smith, 433–459. Englewood, CO: Libraries Unlimited.

Creth, Shelia D. 1986. *Effective On-the-Job Training*. Chicago and London: American Library Association.

Davis, H. Scott. 1994. *New Employee Orientation: A How-To-Do-It Manual for Librarians*. New York: Neal-Schuman Publishers.

DiMarco, Scott R. 2005. "Practicing the Golden Rule: Creating a Win-Win New Employee Orientation." *College and Research Libraries News* 66 no. 2 (Fall): 110–113.

Durrance, Joan C. 1989. "Reference Success: Does the 55 Percent Rule Tell the Whole Story?" *Library Journal* 114, no. 7 (April 15): 31–36.

Durrance, Joan C. 1995. "Factors That Influence Reference Success: What Makes Questioners Willing to Return?" *Reference Librarian* no. 49/50: 243–265.

Emmick, Nancy J. 1985. "Nonprofessionals on Reference Desks in Academic Libraries." In "Conflicts in Reference Services," edited by Bill Katz and Ruth A. Fraley. *The Reference Librarian,* no. 12 (Spring/Summer): 149–160.

Evans, G. Edward. 2002. *Performance Management and Appraisal: A How-To-Do-It Manual for Librarians.* New York and London: Neal-Schuman Publishers.

Flanagan, Pat, and Lisa R. Horowitz. 2000. "Exploring New Service Models: Can Consolidating Public Service Points Improve Response to Customer Needs?" *Journal of Academic Librarianship* 26, no. 5 (September): 329–338.

Geal, Mandy, and Barry Johnson. 2002. "Management Performance: A Glimpse of the Blindingly Obvious." *Training Journal* (October 1): 24–27. Available: http://www.proquest.com/. Accessed: June 16, 2008.

Genz, Marcella D. 1998. "Working the Reference Desk." *Library Trends* 46, no. 3: 505–525.

Giesecke, Joan, and Beth McNeil. 2005. *Fundamentals of Library Supervision.* Chicago: American Library Association.

Gillaspy, Mary L. 2005. "Factors Affecting the Provision of Consumer Health Information in Public Libraries: The Last Five Years." *Library Trends* 53, no. 3: 480–495.

Goodrich, Jeanne, and Paula M. Singer. 2007. *Human Resources for Results: The Right Person for the Right Job.* Chicago: American Library Association.

Goodson, Carol F. 1997. *The Complete Guide to Performance Standards for Library Personnel.* New York: Neal-Schuman Publishers.

Graves, Karen J. 1998. "Implementation and Evaluation of Information Desk Services Provided by Library Technical Assistants." *Bulletin of the Medical Library Association* 86, no. 4 (October): 475–485.

Grogg, Jill E. 2006. "Introduction." *Library Technology Reports* 42, no. 1: 5–7.

Grogg, Jill E. 2006. "On the Road to the OpenURL." *Library Technology Reports* 42, no. 1: 8–13.

Hammond, Carol. 1992. "Information and Research Support Services: The Reference Librarian and the Information Paraprofessional." *Reference Librarian* no. 37: 91–104.

Jackson, Rebecca. 2002. "Revolution or Evolution: Reference Planning in ARL Libraries." *Reference Services Review* 30, no. 3: 212–228.

Jennerich, Elaine Z., and Edward J. Jennerich. 1997. *The Reference Interview as a Creative Art.* 2nd ed. Englewood, CO: Libraries Unlimited.

Johnson, Peggy. 1996. "Managing Changing Roles: Professional and Paraprofessional Staff in Libraries." *Journal of Library Administration* 22, no. 2/3: 79–99.

Katz, William A. 2002a. *Introduction to Reference Work: Basic Information Services, Volume One.* 8th ed. New York: McGraw-Hill.

Katz, William A. 2002b. *Introduction to Reference Work: Volume Two: Reference Services and Reference Processes.* 8th ed. New York: McGraw-Hill.

LaGuardia, Cheryl. 2003. "The Future of Reference: Get Real!" *Reference Services Review* 31, no. 1: 39–42.

Larson, Jeanette, and Herman L. Totten. 1998. *Model Policies for Small and Medium Public Libraries.* New York: Neal-Schuman Publishers.

Lee, Christopher D. 2006. "Feedback, Not Appraisal." *HRMagazine* 51, no. 11: 111–114.

Lichtenstein, Art A. 1999. "Surviving the Information Explosion: Training Paraprofessionals for Reference Service." *Journal of Educational Media & Library Sciences* 37, no. 2: 125–134.

Lipow, Anne Grodzins. 2003. "The Future of Reference: Point-of-Need Reference Service: No Longer an Afterthought." *Reference Services Review* 31, no. 1: 31–35.

Mager, Robert F. 1975. *Preparing Instructional Objectives.* 2nd ed. Belmont, CA: Fearon Publishers.

Mallory, Mary, and Eric Forte. 2001. "Government Documents and Statistics Sources." In *Reference and Information Services.* 3rd ed., edited by Richard E. Bopp and Linda C. Smith, 537–593. Englewood, CO: Libraries Unlimited.

Mayo, Diane, and Jeanne Goodrich. 2002. *Staffing for Results: A Guide to Working Smarter.* Chicago and London: American Library Association.

McDaniel, Julie Ann, and Judith K. Ohles. 1993. *Training Paraprofessionals for Reference Service: A How-To-Do-It Manual for Librarians.* New York: Neal-Schuman Publishers.

McDonald, John, and Eric F. Van de Verde. 2004. "The Lure of Linking." *Library Journal* 129, no. 6 (April 1): 32–34.

McKinzie, Steve. 2002. "For Ethical Reference, Pare the Paraprofessionals." *American Libraries* 33, no. 9 (October): 42.

McLaughlin, Peter. 2007. "Giving Good Feedback." *Supervision* 68, no. 2: 7–8.

Meola, Marc, and Sam Stormont. 2002. *Starting and Operating Live Virtual Reference Services: A How-To-Do-It Manual for Librarians.* New York: Neal-Schuman Publishers.

Metz, Ruth F. 2001. *Coaching in the Library: A Management Strategy for Achieving Excellence*. Chicago and London: American Library Association.

Miller, Susan. 2001. "Directories." In *Reference and Information Services*. 3rd ed., edited by Richard E. Bopp and Linda C. Smith, 331–356. Englewood, CO: Libraries Unlimited.

Morrison, Gary R., Steven M. Ross, and Jerrold E. Kemp. 2004. *Designing Effective Instruction*. 4th ed. Hoboken, NJ: John Wiley.

Mozenter, Frada, Bridgette T. Sanders, and Carol Bellemy. 2003. "Perspectives on Cross-Training Public Service Staff in the Electronic Age: I Have to Learn to Do What?!" *Journal of Academic Librarianship* 29, no. 6 (November): 399–404.

Murfin, Marjorie E., and Lubomyr R. Wynar. 1977. *Reference Service: An Annotated Bibliographic Guide*. Littleton, CO: Libraries Unlimited.

Napier, Alan. 2003. "Spare-Don't Pare-The Paraprofessionals." *American Libraries* 34, no. 4 (April): 38.

Nelson, Sandra, Ellen Altman, and Diane Mayo. 2000. *Managing for Results: Effective Resource Allocation for Public Libraries*. Chicago and London: American Library Association.

Nelson, Sandra, and June Garcia. 2003. *Creating Policies for Results: From Chaos to Clarity*. Chicago: American Library Association.

Pedzich, Joan. 2000. "Paraprofessionals at the Reference Desk: Training and Documentation." *Legal Reference Services Quarterly* 18, no. 2: 91–99.

Piskurich, George M., Peter Beckschi, and Brandon Hall, eds. 2000. *The ASTD Handbook of Training Design and Delivery: A Comprehensive Guide to Creating and Delivering Training Programs, Instructor-led, Computer-based, or Self-directed*. New York: McGraw-Hill Professional.

Reference and User Services Association Division. Reference Services Section. Management of Reference Committee. 2004. "Guidelines for Behavioral Performance of Reference and Information Service Providers." *Reference and User Services Quarterly* 44 (Fall): 14–17.

Rettig, James. 1996. "Future Reference—'Sired by a Hurricane, Dam'd by an Earthquake.'" *Reference Librarian* no. 54: 75–94.

Riedling, Ann Marlow. 2000. "Great Ideas for Improving Reference Interviews." *The Book Report* 19, no. 3 (November/December): 28–29.

Ronan, Jana. 2003. "The Reference Interview Online." *Reference & User Services Quarterly* 43, no. 1: 43–47.

Ross, Catherine Sheldrick. 2003. "The Reference Interview: Why It Needs to Be Used in Every (Well, Almost Every) Reference Transaction." *Reference and User Services Quarterly* 43(Fall): 38–43.

Ross, Catherine Sheldrick, Kristi Nilsen, and Patricia Dewdney. 2002. *Conducting the Reference Interview: A How-To-Do-It Manual for Librarians*. New York: Neal-Schuman Publishers.

Rubin, Rhea Joyce. 2000. "Defusing the Angry Patron." *Library Mosaics* 11, no. 3 (May/June): 14–15.

Rubin, Richard E. 1991. *Human Resource Management in Libraries: Theory and Practice*. New York: Neal-Schuman Publishers.

St. Clair, Jeffrey W., Rao Aluri, and Maureen Pastine. 1977. "Staffing the Reference Desk: Professionals or Nonprofessionals?" *Journal of Academic Librarianship* 3, no. 3 (July): 149–153.

Stueart, Robert D., and Barbara B. Moran. 2002. *Library and Information Center Management*. 6th ed. Greenwood Village, CO: Libraries Unlimited.

Tenopir, Carol. 2007. "Can Johnny Search?" *Library Journal* 132, no. 2 (February 1): 30.

Tenopir, Carol. 2007. "Quality Still Matters." *Library Journal* 132, no. 8 (May 1): 26.

Todaro, Julie. 2001. "Evaluating Your Program." In *Staff Development: A Practical Guide*. 3rd ed., edited by Elizabeth Fuseler Avery, Terry Dahlin, and Deborah A. Carver, 155–161. Chicago and London: American Library Association.

Trotta, Marcia. 1995. *Successful Staff Development: A How-To-Do-It Manual*. New York: Neal-Schuman Publishers.

Trotta, Marcia. 2006. *Supervising Staff: A How-To-Do-It Manual for Librarians*. New York: Neal-Schuman Publishers.

Tucker, James Gory. 2004. "Getting Down to Business: Library Staff Training." *Reference Services Review* 32, no. 3: 293–301.

Tyckoson, David. 2003. "Reference at Its Core: The Reference Interview." *Reference and User Services Quarterly* 43, no. 1 (Fall): 49–51.

United States Department of Labor. Bureau of Labor Statistiscs. *Occupational Outlook Handbook, 2008–2009 Edition*. Available: www.bls.gov/oco.

Voyles, Jeanne F., and Carol A. Friesen. 2001. "Coaching for Results." In *Staff Development: A Practical Guide*. 3rd ed., edited by Elizabeth Fuseler Avery, Terry Dahlin, and Deborah A. Carver, 83–87. Chicago and London: American Library Association.

Weaver-Meyers, Pat. L. 2001. "Creating Effective Training Programs." In *Staff Development: A Practical Guide*. 3rd ed., edited by Elizabeth Fuseler Avery, Terry Dahlin, and Deborah A. Carver, 125–128. Chicago and London: American Library Association.

Weingart, Sandra J., Carol A. Kochan, and Anne Hedrich. 1998. "Safeguarding Your Investment: Effective Orientation for New Employees." *Library Administration & Management* 12, no. 3 (Summer): 156–158.

Woodard, Beth S. 1995. "Reference Training." In *The Reference Assessment Manual*. Compiled and edited by the Evaluation and Adults Services Committee Management and Operations of Public Services Section, Reference and Adult Services Division (RASD) American Library Association, 67–75. Ann Arbor, MI: The Pieran Press.

Woodard, Beth S. 2001. "Reference Service Improvement: Staff Orientation, Training, and Continuing Education." In *Reference and Information Services,* 3rd ed., edited by Richard E. Bopp and Linda C. Smith, 210–244. Englewood, CO: Libraries Unlimited.

Woodard, Beth S., and Sharon J. Van Der Laan. 1986. "Training Preprofessionals for Reference Service." In "Reference Services Today: From Interview to Burnout." *The Reference Librarian* no. 16 (Winter): 233–254.

Zabel, Diane. 2005a. "Trends in Reference and Public Services: Librarianship and the Role of RUSA: Part One." *Reference and User Services Quarterly* 45, no. 1 (Fall): 7–10.

Zabel, Diane. 2005b. "Trends in Reference and Public Services: Librarianship and the Role of RUSA: Part Two." *Reference and User Services Quarterly* 45, no. 2 (Winter): 104–107.

WEB RESOURCES

American Library Association. Association of Specialized and Cooperative Library Agencies. "Library Services for People with Disabilities Policy." In American Library Association. Association of Specialized and Cooperative Library Agencies (Web site). Chicago, Illinois, April 24, 2007. Available: http://www.ala.org/ala/ascla/asclaissues/libraryservices.cfm. Accessed: August 13, 2008.

American Library Association. Reference and User Services Association. Business Reference and Services Section Education Committee. "Company and Industry Research" portion of "Core Competencies for Business Reference." Available: www.ala.org/ala/rusa/rusaourassoc/rusasections/brass/brassprotools/corecompetencies/corecompetenciescompany.cfm. Accessed: January 20, 2008.

"An Explanation of the Superintendent of Documents Classification System." Available: www.access.gpo.gov/su_docs/fdlp/pubs/explain.html. Accessed: June 15, 2008.

Bill and Melinda Gates Foundation. "Web Site Evaluation Resources." Available: www.webjunction.org/do/DisplayContent?id=1301. Accessed: November 2, 2007.

Dewey Decimal Classification System. Available: www.oclc.org/dewey/about/default.htm. Accessed: November 4, 2007.

Duke University. "Evaluating Web Resources." Available: http://library.duke.edu/services/instruction/libraryguide/evalwebpages.html. Accessed: November 2, 2007.

Healey Library Information Literacy Tutorial. "Module 4: How to Evaluate Information on the Web." Available: www.lib.umb.edu/newtutorial/module4_5.html. Accessed: November 2, 2007.

Johns Hopkins University. The Sheridan Libraries. "Evaluating Information Found on the Internet." Available: www.library.jhu.edu/researchhelp/general/evaluating/. Accessed: November 2, 2007.

Library of Congress Classification Outline. Available: www.loc.gov/catdir/cpso/lcco/. Accessed: November 4, 2007.

INDEX

Page numbers followed by "f" indicate a figure.

ABOUT THE AUTHOR

Pamela Morgan is currently a reference librarian/information consultant at the University of Alabama. Prior to this she worked in a variety of professional positions: cataloging and indexing, running a small corporate library, and nearly a decade of reference experience at a large urban public library (including government publications and business science and technology) before making a career switch to academic librarianship.

Pamela is an active member of the American Library Association's Reference and User Services Association. Her committee work includes the Catalog Use Committee, Management of Reference, and Business Reference in Public Libraries.

Pamela graduated with a Master's of Science in Library and Information Science from the University of Illinois Urbana-Champaign in 1993.